Gorgeous Wool Appliqué

A Visual Guide to Adding Dimension & Unique Embroidery

Deborah Gale Tirico

C&T PUBLISHING

Text, artwork, and photography copyright © 2015 by Deborah Gale Tirico

Photography copyright © 2015 by C&T Publishing, Inc.

Publisher: Amy Marson

Creative Director: Gailen Runge

Art Director: Kristy Zacharias

Editor: S. Michele Fry

Technical Editors: Julie Waldman and Gailen Runge

Cover/Book Designer: April Mostek

Production Coordinators: Jenny Davis and Freesia Pearson Blizard

Production Editor: Alice Mace Nakanishi

Illustrator: Deborah Gale Tirico

Photo Assistant: Mary Peyton Peppo

Subject photography by Diane Petersen, style photography by Nissa Brehmer, and instructional photography by Deborah Gale Tirico and Frank Luca Tirico, unless otherwise noted

Published by C&T Publishing, Inc., P.O. Box 1456, Lafayette, CA 94549

Library of Congress Cataloging-in-Publication Data

Tirico, Deborah Gale, 1953-

 Gorgeous wool appliqué : a visual guide to adding dimension & unique embroidery / Deborah Gale Tirico.

    pages cm

 ISBN 978-1-61745-160-7 (soft cover)

 1. Appliqué--Patterns. 2. Felt work. I. Title.

 TT779.T58 2015

 746.44'5--dc23

                        2015015130

Printed in China

10 9 8 7 6 5 4 3 2 1

Contents

PROJECTS

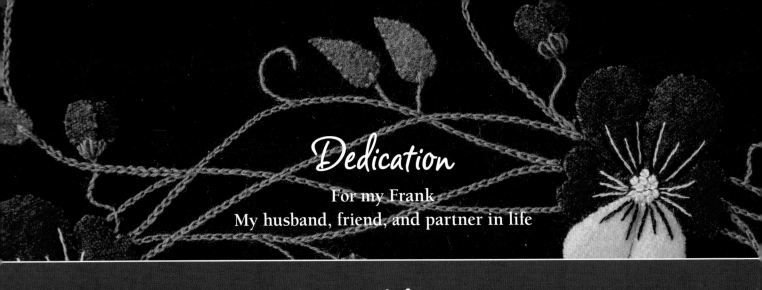

Dedication

For my Frank
My husband, friend, and partner in life

Acknowledgments

So many people in my life have been supportive during my needlework journey, but none more than my mother, Doris, who put a needle in my hand when I was only a small girl and became my most devoted fan.

Big hugs for my husband, Frank, who hand dyed wool, made countless trips to the post office and airport, and never complained when the dining room looked more like a quilt studio.

My dear friend Helene cheerfully traveled with me to classes, shop hops, quilt shows, and embroidery seminars, sharing the fabrics and threads and always making it more fun.

I am grateful to my amazingly supportive sisters, Cindy, Carol, Janet, and Robin, who have oohed and aahed at every showing of my work since I was a teenager.

I must also recognize my lifelong friend and colleague Mari. Mari's encouragement and support was unwavering as she held the fort at Gemini Studio. Many thanks!

I also wish to thank all my pilot students for reading directions, making excellent suggestions, and helping me become a better instructor.

Foreword

My sister, Deb, has always been a stitcher. Her talent with a needle showed itself early and came seemingly out of nowhere. "I don't know where she learned how to do this," our astonished mother would say about one of her creations. "She's just a little girl and everything she does is beautiful!"

Deb was a teenager when the hippie culture brought gauzy peasant blouses, fringed miniskirts, and embroidered jeans into our home. Styles were changing, and Deb, always the savvy older sister, knew exactly how to make a fashion statement. I remember her helping me jazz up my jeans by showing me how to embroider the bottom of my bell-bottoms. First she drew the design using a pen. Next, she patiently showed me how to embroider the flowers, curlicues, and iconic peace symbols that were the mainstays back then. How I loved the chain stitch that meandered all along the hemline, the glossy satin stitch of the daisies, and the French knots that dotted the design like exclamation points. At school, my jeans were a hit!

Embroidery became Deb's therapy. The week before her wedding, when the house was in a flurry of preparations and plans, Deb was squirreled away in the den embroidering sachet pillows as gifts for her bridal attendants. Her work was always beautiful, but now it was also an expression from the heart. I played the piano, so my sachet displayed an intricately embroidered keyboard; the sewer in the family had a sewing machine on hers; and the sister who accompanied us at campfire sing-alongs had a guitar on hers.

Years later, at a family retreat at Lake George, New York, Deb organized a quilting class. The fact that we were all novices didn't deter her. She deftly distributed all the materials we needed to make a simple quilted potholder and then proceeded to show us how to go about making it. I remember marveling at her instructional style. She was so confident and so patient—a born teacher. When we faltered, she simply redirected us. She knew the end result would be pretty—too pretty, in fact, to use. I hung it on the wall.

Now, Deb has embarked on another creative journey with this collection of unique designs to stitch. Each design began as an idea. The result is where Deb's curiosity, creativity, and passion ultimately led her. I hope you enjoy stitching these designs as much as she enjoyed creating them. Happy stitching!

—Janet Aaronson
Somerville, New Jersey

Introduction

As an avid fan of appliqué I have always been intrigued with wool penny rugs and their construction and history. I was creating my own designs using raw-edged fabric and the blanket stitch when I was just 10 years old, and to this day it remains one of my favorite stitching methods.

Unlike many designs in felted wool today, my work is not primitive in design. Coming from a formal appliqué background, I use matching wool threads and dimensional appliqué methods, and I embellish my work with embroidery. As a result, my designs are sophisticated and dimensional and offer clarity to their subject, making them quite distinctive.

The organic and forgiving nature of felted wool allows me to sculpt my table rugs and home fashion accessories, bringing a lush, colorful accent to any room. My needle-slanting technique and methods for marking embroidery guides will appeal to the embroiderer, the quilter, and any lover of hand sewing.

The projects in this book are functional, are quick to stitch, and make wonderful gifts. The patterns include both small and large projects that can be completed on vacation, while traveling, in between larger projects, or as quick gifts for friends.

My inspiration for these designs comes from a variety of subjects, and I have included them so that you, too, may begin to think about what appeals to you designwise in the world and then translate those things into sculpted wool creations of your own.

Happy stitching!

—Deborah Gale Tirico

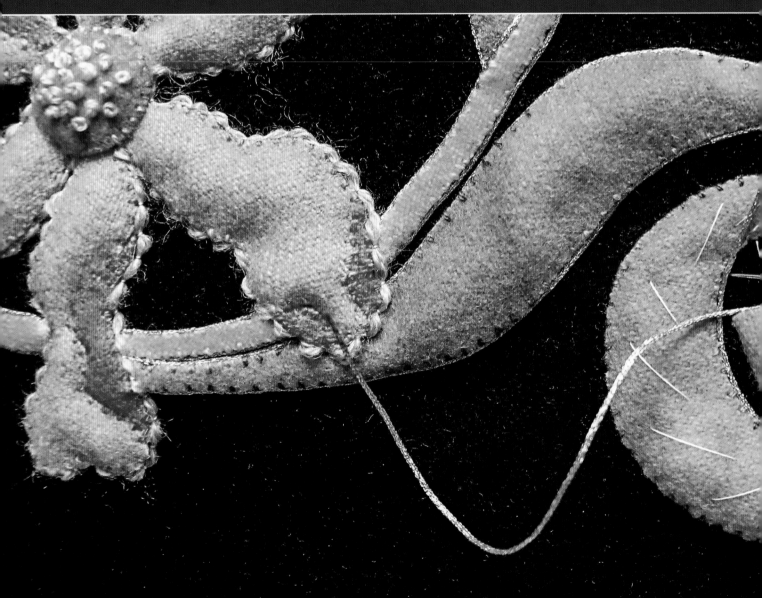

PREPARING FOR SUCCESS

The Basics

ABOUT FELTED WOOL

I am often asked about felted wool, and this is how I explain the differences in wool fabric.

Felted wool is actually woven wool yardage that has a weft and a warp. When this yardage is felted, it is shrunk in hot water followed by high-heat drying, causing it to constrict and become dense. This fabric is easy to needle because the holes between the warp and weft remain. Once felted, woven wool yardage will not easily fray.

Wool felt is made from wool roving, which is pressed into sheets using hot water and high heat, causing it to become dense. This fabric is a bit more difficult to needle because unlike a woven fabric it has no holes.

Some wool felt is actually a blend of 70% wool and 30% polyester and behaves well in a variety of applications because it has absolutely no fray.

Craft felt is made from 100% synthetic materials. Some is even made using recycled plastic bottles ... a much different feel and form.

I use felted wool for all my base fabrics and the majority of my appliqué fabrics. My process is to felt all my own base fabrics (white, off-white, and black), dye and overdye some of my own colors when I am unable to procure suitable colors, and buy from felted wool houses all the colors that are used in smaller pieces.

I hope your journey using this book will encourage you to felt your own wool, experiment with a bit of dyeing and overdyeing, and see how beautifully these natural fibers needle and behave as you sculpt your own creations.

FELTING WOOL

Wool yardage can be felted by washing it with hot water and a little detergent and then drying it at high heat. The fabric will shrink nicely and eliminate the large amount of fraying that would result from using wool yardage that is not felted.

Fabrics from wool clothing can also be felted, but use some caution when selecting them. The following guidelines will help in choosing fabrics to recycle and use for felted wool creations.

- Always look for a label identifying the fabric as 100% wool.

- Do not use wool gabardine because it has many more warp than weft yarns and will not felt evenly.

- Melton wool, a heavy cloth that is tightly woven and finished with a smooth face concealing the weave, is often used for overcoats. This wool is excellent for use in appliqués and does not require felting.

> ### NOTE
> Wool yardage typically comes in a 58″ width; it will shrink a few inches when felted. The supply lists for the projects in this book are based on this standard. If you are using felt made from clothing, you'll need to do a little experimenting to determine the amount of wool needed.

THREADS

Wool Thread

There are many different types of wool thread, which can be found in skeins or on spools. Wool thread is traditionally used in crewel embroidery and is often referred to as crewel thread. It ranges from the weight of two-ply lace-weight yarn to a much finer thread on a spool and can be found in embroidery and needlepoint shops and online. Wool thread does not need to be split but is used as is.

Cotton Floss

Cotton floss comes in six-stranded skeins and is generally split (called stripping) to allow the stitcher to decide how thick the embroidery should be. In the majority of the designs in this book, floss is used in a single strand and is therefore split.

Perle Cotton

Perle cotton is a single-stranded cotton thread that has a bit of a shine and comes in three weights: #5, #8, and #12, with the latter being the thinnest. Perle cotton is found in skeins and wrapped balls and is often used for decorative embellishment, blanket-stitched edges, and twisted cord.

TOOLS AND SUPPLIES

NEEDLES   Use crewel needles in a variety of different sizes when working with felted wool appliqué. When basting or making embroidery guides, use a straw needle or a milliners #11.

TWEEZERS   This is a critical tool for the placement of shapes under the placement guide.

ACETATE   For placement guides, use 8-mil acetate, which should be available on the bolt at your local fabric store.

TISSUE   Tissue is available at most stores that carry wrapping paper. Select tissue paper used for gift wrapping when marking your embroidery lines. You can also find larger pieces of tissue paper at office supply stores.

SCISSORS   Use scissors with short blades and large handles for the best results when cutting small shapes. Pinking shears are also used in one of the projects to create a zigzag edge to an appliquéd flower.

GLUE   You can baste with glue instead of stitches to hold very small appliqué pieces in place while doing the appliqué stitch. My favorite glue is Roxanne Glue-Baste-It, which has a great applicator tip.

Prework

Before beginning an appliqué project we prepare the frame of the base fabric; a veil or placement guide; and, if there will be a good deal of embroidery, an embroidery guide. This work involves tracing the pattern and creating an environment that will make the appliqué and embroidery work accurate, easier to complete, and fun. The following describes the process for creating each of these important tools.

The work you do here in preparing to appliqué will actually make the entire project go smoothly, so take your time and be careful to make accurate tracings. Although not the most fun, this work is the most critical in the execution of accurately placed embroidery. Later on you will be grateful to have a clearly defined placement guide for your appliqué shapes. As you are chainstitching away, the wonderful running-stitch guide will mark your path and make the embroidery not only fun but extremely accurate.

MARKING THE BASE SHAPE

Whatever the final shape of your project—a square, a circle, an oval, whatever—it is important to mark the edges in order to center the appliqué design accurately. When marking the base for wool projects, I use a freezer-paper pattern and a pen. When marking for a white field, I use a Micron archival pen. When marking for a black field, I use a white gel pen.

1. Trace the pattern for the project base onto the flat (not shiny) side of a piece of freezer paper.

2. Cut out the shape and iron it onto the wool fabric with a hot iron, shiny side down.

3. Using a white gel pen or black Micron archival pen, trace a line around the outside of the freezer-paper pattern onto the wool fabric.

4. Remove the freezer paper. You will have a line marking the edge of the design area, which can be cut away once the appliqué and embroidery are completed. Do not cut the base fabric shape out until you are finished with your appliqué and embroidery, as the base and the backing will be cut together.

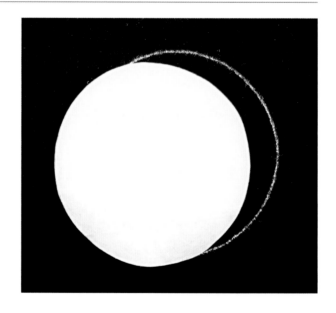

5. Cut the base shape from the wool yardage so that there will be less fabric weight to deal with as you work. For the base shape, cut slightly larger than your marked line all the way around; for the smaller shapes, cut ⅛" to ¼" larger all the way around.

CREATING A PLACEMENT GUIDE

Positioning the Appliqué Shapes

1. Position a piece of clear plastic acetate over the pattern, and secure it with small pieces of tape, to avoid slippage. Eight-mil acetate can be found at craft and fabric stores in the home fabrics department. This type of acetate is often used for table covers and slipcovers.

2. Using a thin (not ultrathin) Sharpie marker, trace the lines of the design with as much detail as possible. Be sure to trace the outer shape of the item as well, so you will be able to position the design accurately on the base fabric. This will be your master placement guide for the appliqué.

tip

Write your name or the word yes on the right side of the acetate so you will not inadvertently use it upside down. (Trust me—it's easy to do.)

tip: Hinging a Guide

Hinging the placement guide to the top of the base allows it to be easily flipped up and down so you can place the appliqué shapes and make adjustments. To do this, position the acetate placement guide on the felted wool base, lining up the top and right sides. Pin at the top edge with at least three pins. The pins should be placed horizontally.

CREATING EMBROIDERY GUIDES

Marking the Pattern on Tissue Paper for Transfer

Embroidery guides are a great comfort when the design includes curling vines and stems. Guides enable focus and concentration on the development of an even pace in stitching, resulting in even, attractive work. Following an embroidery guide allows the stitcher to know exactly where to place the needle next, which makes embroidery even more enjoyable. The following section details how to create an embroidery guide.

1. Position a piece of tissue paper over the pattern and, using a pencil, carefully trace the vines, stems, and all lines to be embroidered onto this paper. Indicate every line that will be embroidered. Indicate the outside shape of the item (be it a table rug, pillow, or pincushion, the exterior shape line is important); this ensures that you can position the pattern correctly on the base fabric. If you like, you can indicate the outline of the other shapes to aid you in placing the tissue correctly later. Refer to the image to be sure you have indicated every embroidered line. Include top, bottom, right, and left notations also, as this will make things much easier later.

tip

A pencil is best for the initial tracing, as it will not bleed through the tissue and mark the pattern below.

2. Mark the right side of the tissue by writing your name.

3. Remove the pattern from below the tissue and retrace the pencil lines with pen so you will have a clear indication when placing the tissue on the base felted wool.

4. Position the marked tissue paper on the base fabric (which should already be marked with the outside line), making sure that the outside lines on the tissue paper line up with the outside lines on the fabric. Pin in place, avoiding the traced lines to be embroidered.

5. Using cotton thread that matches the color of the thread you will use to embroider, stitch running stitches, as tiny as possible, through the pencil lines onto the wool base. (You will ultimately embroider over these lines with wool thread, covering them.) Begin and end with a backstitch, leaving a tail of approximately 1″ at either end. Note that you do not need to create guidelines for embroidery that will be on top of appliqué pieces.

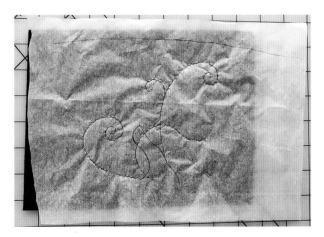

6. Rip the tissue away in quick motions toward the stitched line. Use tweezers to remove any residual tissue from the stitches. If there are any loops in the lines of stitching, pull on the tails at either end to smooth them. Stretching the wool in both directions will generally smooth out any loops.

7. When you are satisfied with the stitching, cut the tails at either end flush with the wool base. You are now ready to embroider over this guide.

Tips for Stitching through Tissue Paper

- Make sure your pins are 3″ apart to prevent slippage while stitching.

- Use a long, thin needle such as a milliners or straw needle.

- The thread length should be less than twice the distance from your fingertips to the crease in your elbow.

- Use a backstitch at the beginning and end of each line. Do not use knots.

- Try to fill the needle with at least three stitches before drawing the thread through.

- After every few stitches, you can roll the needle toward you to uncurl the thread; this will prevent knots.

- If your thread knots, slip the needle inside the loop of the knot and pull to the right to unknot.

- Manipulate and move the fabric between your fingers to make the stitching easier.

EMBROIDERY OVER RUNNING STITCH GUIDELINES

Use a length of thread that is less than twice the distance from your fingertips to your elbow crease. Wool thread is stressed when it is run through wool fabric, so shorter threads that change position on the needle as you sew will work best. The rule of thumb when covering basting stitches with a stem stitch (page 94) is to enter the fabric slightly to the left of the guide stitch and exit slightly to the right of the guide.

MAKING FREEZER-PAPER PATTERNS

1. Trace the pattern pieces for sections or elements as you go. Using this process, you will get to the sewing quickly, and ultimately not lose small pieces. You won't find them later on your elbow or on the dog!

2. Trace the pattern pieces onto the flat (not shiny) side of a piece of freezer paper. Iron the freezer-paper patterns, shiny side down, onto the felted wool fabric, grouping pattern pieces of the same color. It's a good idea to rough cut the traced freezer-paper patterns and arrange them on the felted wool fabric before pressing and ironing. This is helpful if you have a small piece of fabric and want to be sure everything will fit.

3. Rough cut the freezer-paper patterns for each piece, trimming close to, but not on, the cutting line so you can cut out each piece separately. This will make cutting more accurate, as you will not have the weight of the fabric pulling or weighing as you cut. Keep the pieces for each color separated so they'll be easier to sort out when you're ready to stitch.

4. Using a sharp pair of scissors, cut out each shape using the freezer-paper tracing line as your guide, but do not remove the freezer paper. You may wish to key the pieces to your pattern placement guide, using letters or numbers, to avoid confusion later.

Cutting Tools and Tips

• When cutting small pieces (anything under 4″), a small blade is recommended. I personally use scissors with a blade shorter than 2″ and large comfortable handles, which makes cutting fun, comfortable, and easy. Avoid running with them, however.

• When cutting small pieces, try to have your scissors maintain contact with the fabric at all times. As you open the scissors, press the fabric into the tool and maintain contact. This prevents the "jaggies." As you cut using your dominant hand, rotate the fabric piece with your opposite hand.

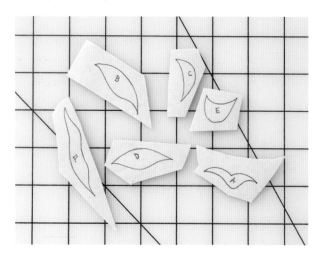

Appliquéing
with Felted Wool

A Different Approach

Traditional appliqué uses a sewing motion, catching a fiber or two of cotton fabric in a single needle-down, needle-up motion, pulling tight so the stitch will ultimately disappear.

When appliquéing with felted wool, you will use the *opposite* motion. Draw your needle up from the base near the edge of the felted wool shape and carefully place the down stitch directly opposite from the needle-up position. The stitch will always show, so careful placement is critical. Using matching threads will allow the stitch to *disappear* as much as possible, and using wool thread will further ensure that the thread will stick to the fabric. Wool thread and wool fabric have surface fibers that will intermingle, thereby enabling them to stay in position.

For the best result use a *light* hand and a stab-stitch motion to appliqué wool. With the stab stitch, your stitches will be accurate and you can carefully work around any frays. Pull the thread until a small loop remains and then gently complete the stitch, allowing the thread to rest lightly on the side of the appliqué piece. Do not pull it tight or the work will have a bunched edge effect.

> **NOTE**
> Using a light hand or light touch is critical to success with my felted wool appliqué techniques. When you see the feather icon throughout this book, remember to work with a gentle hand.

When you come to a point, stitch on one side of it and then the other. Never stitch in the tip of a point or you will encourage fraying, and the point will not remain clean and sharp. In other words, ignore the points.

THE TACK STITCH

The basic stitch I use for felted wool appliqué is the tack stitch. It creates a straight stitch on the top of the project while the thread moves diagonally underneath. The needle goes in and out of the fabric straight up and straight down, which is called *stab stitching*.

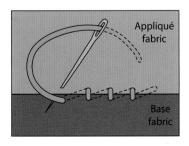

Appliqué fabric

Base fabric

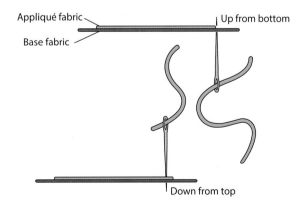

Appliqué fabric

Base fabric

Up from bottom

Down from top

ADDING DIMENSION

A variety of methods can be used to add dimension to your work, including stuffing, trapunto, layering, and needle-slanting techniques. A felted wool appliqué piece will show off its dimensions when side lit, just as quilts show their quilting lines best with certain angles of light.

Stuffing

Any piece can be slightly stuffed for added dimension. This works especially well with fruit. Jacobean Pillow (page 55) incorporates stuffing for the pomegranate and the center of the blue fantasy flower.

Trapunto

From the Italian word meaning "to quilt," trapunto is a method of quilting that is also called *stuffed technique*. A puffy, decorative feature, trapunto uses at least two layers, the underside of which is slit and padded, producing a raised surface on the quilt. The pieces in this book do not use trapunto, but you could use this technique if you wish on Jacobean Pillow (page 55).

Layering

Layering pieces of felted wool also creates a dimensional effect. Harvest Penny Rug (page 20) uses layering techniques, making the pumpkin appear sculpted and realistic. This is accomplished by layering four pieces and appliquéing through all the layers as you add each piece.

Needle Slanting

Needle slanting is my signature technique used for almost all the appliqué pieces in this book. You will discover when appliquéing with wool that if you bring your needle up just shy of the edge in a slanting motion and then down perpendicular to the needle-up motion, the edge of the piece will be forced into a slight puff. This is similar to the tack stitch except that the needle goes up and down at a slight angle.

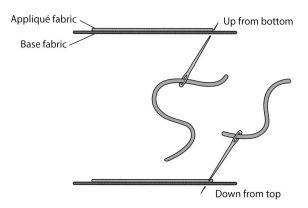

Appliqué fabric — Up from bottom
Base fabric — Down from top

This technique provides a successful treatment for adding dimension to any piece, but it can be overdone—so remember to keep your hands very light when stitching and make all your slanting stitches slight. Overdoing this technique will result in a puckered edge. I further recommend that you turn the work often so that each edge to be appliquéd is positioned to be easily stitched from right to left. (If you are left-handed, you will be stitching from left to right!)

Perfect Pennies

Penny rugs are said to have been born around the time of the Civil War, when resourceful quiltmakers recycled pieces of wool clothing to decorate mats and runners. They used coins or pennies as templates. Those coin-sized salvaged wool pieces were usually laid out in a design on top of a larger piece of fabric and sewn on, often with a blanket stitch, a layer at a time. Early penny rugs were used as table and mantel coverings or to protect fine carpets hearthside. I love the look of pennies as borders, and they are featured on Harvest Penny Rug (page 20) and Nutcracker Penny Rug (page 29). Here's how I create perfect pennies.

1. Using template plastic and the penny patterns (pages 26 and 38), create master templates for the large and small pennies by tracing onto the plastic and then carefully cutting out the circles.

2. Use these templates to trace freezer-paper patterns for the number of small pennies and large pennies needed for the project. Trace them onto the flat (not shiny) side of the freezer paper.

3. Rough cut the pennies, and then cut out each one individually without the bulk of the fabric pulling on your work. Leave the freezer paper on the pieces until you are ready to use them. This will help make sure they keep their shape until they are ready for use.

4. Center a small penny on a large penny, and then pin and baste in place using cotton thread. Baste using large sweeping stitches (do not use knots) and leave most of the thread on the top. (Using this method makes it easy to cut away the basting stitches and pull them out when the appliqué is complete.)

tip

These pieces can easily slip as you stitch, creating a skewed penny, so do not use a shortcut here. Baste! (See Basting, page 18.)

5. Using a length of wool thread, tackstitch the top penny in place. Remove the basting.

6. Place the assembled piece from Step 5 on the penny back and baste these 2 together.

7. Using a length of perle cotton #8, blanket stitch along the outside edge. Remove the basting.

Embrace the Basting

Disciplined basting techniques can help enhance your enjoyment of the work. I have developed a method of basting that eliminates thread from the appliqué edge and holds the tails of the thread. It also makes removal of the basting stitches quick and easy.

1. Thread a milliners needle with a length of white cotton thread; do *not* knot it.

2. Make a large stitch at the top of the penny, leaving a 1″ tail.

3. Make a second stitch on top of the first, anchoring the tail under the stitch. Follow with additional large stitches over the thread tail.

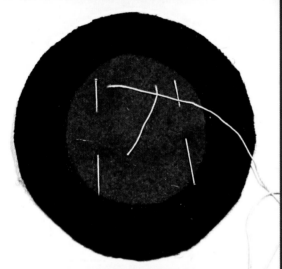

4. Finish as you began, with a stitch on top of the last stitch, and run your needle up under the stitches to anchor the tail; then cut the thread.

5. The penny is now basted with the tails anchored and out of the way of the appliqué stitches. Once the appliqué is complete, it will be easy to snip the threads and remove the basting stitches.

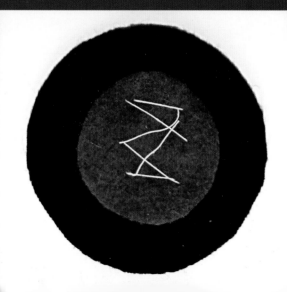

THE TABLE RUGS

Harvest

Penny Rug

Finished rug:
33½″ × 19″

Inspiration

When I realized one of my favorite fabric manufacturers was going to discontinue a much-loved line of overdyed felted wool, I decided to invest in a few bolts of my favorite colors. The fabric arrived at my office and one of my colleagues looked at the bolt of orange overdyed fabric and said, "Oooooh, looks like pumpkin." This caused an idea to spring to mind—to create a harvest table rug—and I began to search the Internet for images. I created this design after researching pumpkins, acorns, and cranberries, and I set out to make a table rug.

SUPPLIES

- 1¼ yards black felted wool
- Fat quarter of dark green felted wool (color-saturated overdyed)
- Fat eighth of gold felted wool (color-saturated overdyed)
- Scrap pieces of yellow, red, light green, and brown felted wool
- Crewel-weight wool threads to match all felted wool colors

- Crewel-weight dark brown and light brown wool thread for pumpkin stem embellishment
- Black perle cotton #8
- Template plastic
- Crewel and tapestry needles
- Burgundy floss for flower centers

Prework

For details on marking the base fabric and making guides, see The Basics (page 8).

1. Prepare the base shape (page 10).

2. Create a placement guide (page 11).

3. Create an embroidery guide (page 12).

Make Freezer-Paper Patterns

1. Trace all the pattern pieces for the pumpkin, leaves, flowers, acorn, and berries onto the flat (not shiny) side of the freezer paper.

2. Group the pieces by color so you can iron the shapes of the same color to the selected fabrics. Rough cut the freezer-paper patterns by color, trimming close to, but not on, the cutting line for each group of pieces.

3. Iron the freezer-paper patterns, shiny side down, onto the orange, dark green, light green, yellow, red, and brown felted wool.

> **NOTE**
>
> When you position the pumpkin pieces using overdyed fabric, you may want to try to "fussy cut" to create a shaded effect. Use the darker colors for the edges to create this effect. Use a dark section of the gold felted wool for the acorn bottom and a light section for the acorn cap.

4. Cut out all the shapes but do not remove the freezer paper.

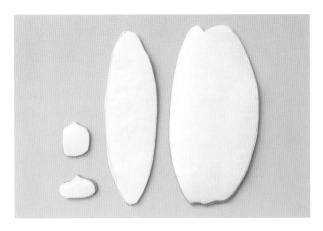

 tip

Key the pieces to your pattern placement guide, using letters or numbers, to avoid confusion later. This will be especially important on the underleaf pieces, which are a lighter green. The new-growth leaves should be light green.

Cut Out the Pennies

 tip

Make sure your scissors are sharp.

Cut out the pieces using the freezer-paper trace line as your guide. Do not remove the paper until you are ready to place the pieces on the base. You will need 56 black pennies and 28 green pennies. Pennies are good to take to your sewing group, on a flight, or anywhere that portable needlework is convenient.

Assemble the Pumpkin

1. Peel the freezer paper away and place the pumpkin shapes on top of each other as indicated on the placement guide.

2. Using the clear plastic placement guide, position and pin the pieces as indicated to prevent them from shifting as you baste them to the background and to each other. Using a light-colored sewing thread, baste these shapes in place. Remove the pins as you baste.

3. Using a length of matching wool thread, tackstitch the pumpkin in place, starting at the outer edge and stitching the sides of each shape in place. Be sure to go through all the layers of the felted wool with your needle to anchor the pumpkin in place. Remove the basting stitches.

> **tip**
>
> *A stab-stitching action is best for this work, as the layers are thick. This process will serve to strengthen and weight the entire piece. (See The Tack Stitch, page 15.)*

4. Position the stem at the top of the pumpkin and place the base of the stem snug against the pumpkin top. Pin, baste, and tackstitch the stem in place with matching wool thread according to the placement guide.

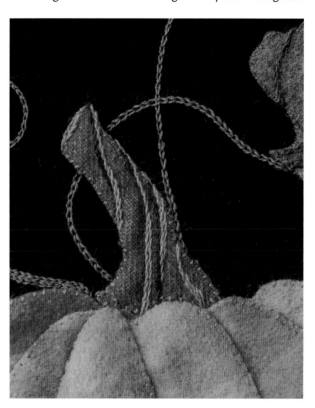

Appliqué the Leaves, Berries, and Flowers

Leaves are constructed using 2 shades of green wool, with the lighter shade indicating the leaf underside.

1. Find the 2 pieces that make the leaf to the immediate right of the pumpkin stem. Peel the freezer paper away and place the pieces according to the placement guide. Pin and baste them in place.

2. Using a length of matching wool thread, tackstitch the dark green leaf first. Place the leaf underside piece snug against the upper leaf and tackstitch this piece in place using lighter green thread.

> **tip**
>
> *Avoid making stitches on the points of any pieces.*

3. Peel and position the flowers, berries, and berry leaves in place according to the placement guide. For smaller pieces, use a drop of glue to baste and tweezers to position the pieces snugly.

4. Visually double-check the positioning to be sure the placement pleases you. With matching wool thread, tackstitch the berries, leaves, and flowers.

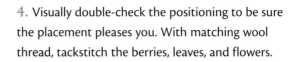

Appliqué the Acorn

1. Peel and position the acorn and acorn cap according to the placement guide. You can baste with thread or a drop of glue, as you wish.

2. Tackstitch with matching threads.

Embellish

• Leaves and flower petals are embellished using wool thread and straight stitches.

• Vines and the pumpkin stem are embellished using wool thread and a chain stitch. The vines appear thicker in some areas because the rows of chain stitches are doubled or tripled, as indicated in the pattern. The vine with the tiny leaves is created using a stem stitch to make it thinner. (There are 3 tiny vines total.)

• The cranberries feature 4 lazy daisy stitches in wool thread.

• The pumpkin flower centers are made with 2 strands of burgundy floss for the colonial knots in the center and 1 strand of burgundy floss for the seed stitches.

• The acorn cap features fly stitches in a random pattern.

Assemble the Rug

BACK THE RUG

1. Place the rug top on a piece of wool large enough to accommodate the rug base and baste the 2 pieces securely around the edge, about ½" *inside* the marked white line that you made at the very beginning.

2. Cut both pieces together just inside the white line, so any trace of the line will be removed and your pattern will be accurate.

3. Using a length of black perle cotton #8, stitch the edges of the top and back together with a blanket stitch (page 93).

MAKE THE PENNIES

1. Create templates for the large and small pennies from template plastic. Use these templates to make freezer-paper patterns for the 28 small pennies and the 56 large pennies, tracing them onto the flat (not shiny) side of the freezer paper.

2. Group these pennies by color, which will make it easy to press them onto the green and black wool.

3. Cut out the pennies but leave the freezer paper on until you are ready to use them.

4. Baste and then tackstitch a green penny to the center of a black penny. Baste and then buttonhole stitch this combination penny to another black penny.

5. Assemble all the pennies (see Perfect Pennies, page 17).

ATTACH THE PENNIES

1. Carefully place the pennies along the outside edge of the rug and pin them in place.

2. Using basic white sewing thread, baste the pennies in place around the edge of the rug.

3. With black quilting thread, whipstitch (page 94) the perle cotton threads together, securing the pennies to each other and to the rug base.

A

D

J

F

C

B

H

I

G

E

Dark green pieces

Note: Shaded areas show where light green pieces fit; refer to light green pieces (page 27) and photos for this project.

K

L

For pennies, cut 28.

Black

For pennies, cut 56.

Gold

For acorn base, cut from a darker area of wool.

For acorn cap, cut from a lighter area of wool.

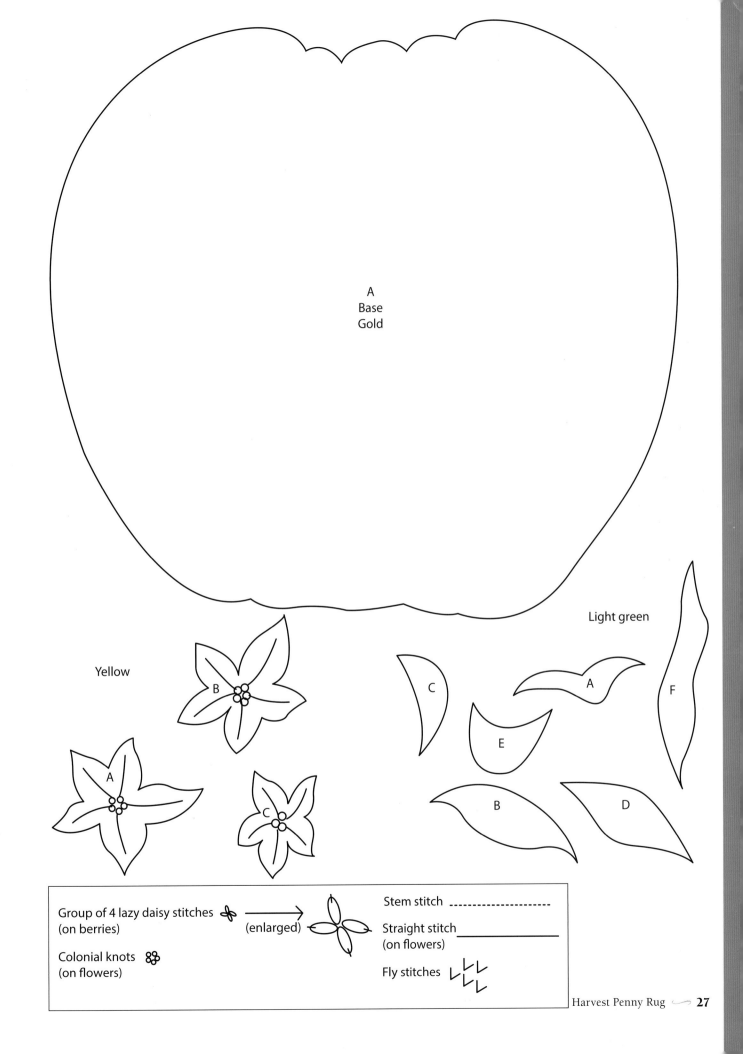

A
Base
Gold

Light green

Yellow

B

C

A

F

E

A

C

B

D

Group of 4 lazy daisy stitches
(on berries)

(enlarged)

Stem stitch ----------------------

Straight stitch _____
(on flowers)

Colonial knots
(on flowers)

Fly stitches

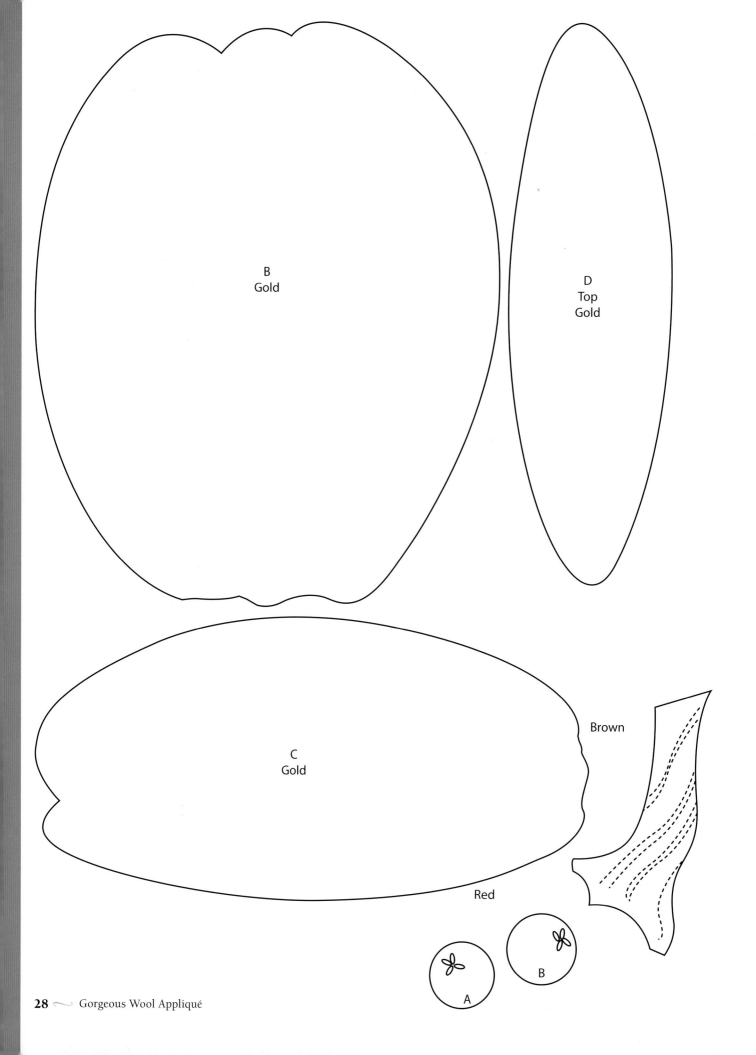

B
Gold

D
Top
Gold

C
Gold

Brown

Red

A

B

Nutcracker
Penny Rug

Finished rug: 33½″ × 19″

When I was a girl I attended ballet academy and performed in the Nutcracker every Christmas season for years. Since then, nutcrackers have always meant Christmas for me. So when asked by one of my students to create a holiday table rug design, this was my only choice. When I finalized the design (after looking at way too many nutcrackers), the soldier looked a bit lonely, and so I added the evergreen bough and pinecones, which completed the design. When I added this table rug to my dining room table, the entire room seemed decked out for the holidays.

SUPPLIES

- Freezer paper for pattern making

- Clear acetate for placement guide

- 1¼ yards white felted wool for base and pennies

- Fat quarter each of red and black felted wool

- Scraps of mustard yellow, blue, green, light peach, white, and gray felted wool

- Wool threads to match all felted wool colors

- Off-white perle cotton #8

- Fine thread in silver and gold for jacket and boot lace embellishment

- Beads for jacket buttons and crown embellishment

- Crewel and tapestry needles

- Blush to color the cheeks

Prework

For details on marking the shapes and making guides, see The Basics (page 8).

1. Mark the base shape (page 10).

2. Create a placement guide (page 11).

3. Create an embroidery guide (page 12).

Embroider, Cut, and Appliqué

EMBROIDER THE PINE VINE

Create a stitching guide for the vines using green sewing thread.

Using a length of green wool thread, stem stitch (page 94) the vines over the stitching guides.

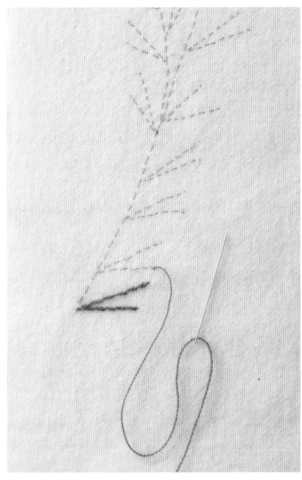

> **NOTE**
>
> Remember to use a length of thread that is less than twice the distance from your fingertips to your elbow crease. Wool thread is stressed when it is run through wool fabric, so shorter threads will work better.

tip

Thread a few needles so you will be able to develop a rhythm and not have to stop to thread.

MAKE THE PENNIES

1. Create plastic templates for the large and small penny patterns (page 17).

2. Use these templates to make freezer-paper patterns for 28 small pennies and 56 large pennies. Trace them onto the dull (not shiny) side of the freezer paper. Group these pennies by color, which will make it easy to press them onto the red and white wool.

3. Cut out the pennies but leave the freezer paper on until you are ready to use them.

4. Center a red penny on a white penny and baste in place.

As you stitch these pieces they can easily slip, creating a skewed penny, so do not use a shortcut here. Baste!

5. Using a length of red wool thread, tackstitch the red penny in place. Remove the basting.

6. Place the assembled penny from Step 5 on another white penny and baste those together. Using a length of off-white perle cotton, blanket stitch these pennies together along the edge.

MAKE FREEZER-PAPER PATTERNS

1. Using a pencil or pen, trace all the pattern pieces for the nutcracker onto the flat (not shiny) side of the freezer paper. Group the pieces by color so you can iron the shapes of the same color to the selected fabric.

2. Iron the freezer-paper patterns, shiny side down, onto the felted wool fabric. Rough cut the freezer-paper patterns by color, trimming close to, but not on, the cutting line for each piece so you can basically trim each piece separately. This will make cutting more accurate, as you will not have the weight of the fabric pulling.

3. Cut out each shape using the freezer-paper line as your guide, but do not remove the freezer paper. You may wish to key the pieces to your pattern placement guide, using letters or numbers, to avoid confusion later.

POSITION THE APPLIQUÉ

Hinge the placement guide. (During the project, the acetate guide will be removed for stitching and repositioned and pinned to add additional shapes. Using this guide will ensure the accuracy of the design. Hinging will allow you to get it back into the same place multiple times.)

POSITION THE FIGURE

Find the following pieces and pin and baste them into position in the following order:

• Blue, mustard yellow, and green hat pieces

• Peach face and black hair pieces

• Green collar, red main jacket piece, and green trim at bottom of jacket

• Blue and mustard yellow leg pieces

• Black boot pieces

These pieces will create the base for the soldier, and getting them lined up and basted tightly into position is critical. When appliquéing with felted wool fabric, pieces tend to shift and move, so use a light hand when stitching.

1. Using a tack stitch and the needle-slanting technique, appliqué the pieces in the order indicated. The order will help maintain a straight figure.

- Collar and jacket

- Legs and boots
  Leave the outside edge of the leg pieces unstitched.

- Hat and face

The hat will be layered and the top pieces will anchor the pieces underneath, so appliqué only the edges of the top pieces.

2. Appliqué the hair pieces. Press them toward the head to get them snug against the face when stitching.

LAYER THE PIECES

The Face

1. Position the eyes, eyeballs, eyebrows, nose, and mustache on the face according to the placement guide.

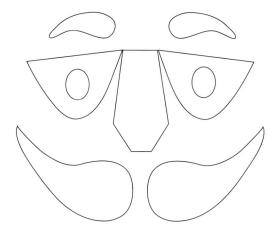

2. Baste these pieces and tackstitch them with a light hand using the needle-slanting technique to create dimension in the face.

tip

When appliquéing the face pieces, bring your needle all the way through to the back; it will give the piece additional support.

3. Apply blush to the cheeks as a finishing touch. Yes, real powder makeup. It works great.

The Teeth

The most effective way to make the teeth is to satin stitch (page 94) them using white wool thread.

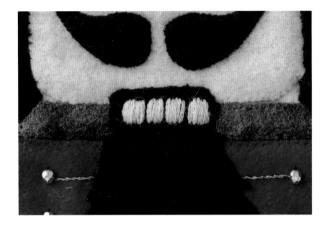

The Beard and Jacket

1. Add the belt pieces to the jacket.

2. Embroider the button embellishments with a stem stitch. You can use a tissue-paper embroidery guide if you wish. (See Making an Embroidery Guide, page 12.)

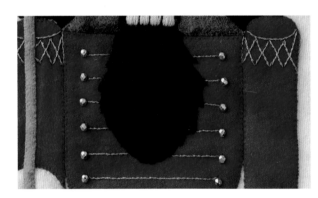

3. Appliqué the beard.

Hints

• The pieces should be needled all the way through to the bottom using the needle-slanting technique.

• Leave the green jacket center edges open for additional dimension.

• Stitches "linking" the button chains go under the beard.

The Legs

Add the green stripes to the legs using the needle-slanting technique. Carefully overlap the outside edge slightly in order to both anchor and hide the blue edge.

The Boot Embellishments

1. Embroider the boots with silver braid using a stem stitch.

2. Add a colonial knot at each end to indicate a rivet.

3. Use white basting thread to create guidelines and stem stitch next to them to be sure the laces are lined up.

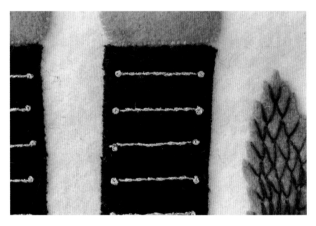

The Arms and Hands

1. Add the arms, hands, and cuff pieces. Pin and then baste them before tackstitching them in place.

2. Embellish the shoulders with gold braid in a cross-hatched design. If you like, use white thread to create a guideline for the top and bottom of the stitching to keep a uniform look.

The Battle-Ax

Position and baste the pieces of the battle-ax, which overlaps the hair, arm, and hand. Be careful to make the handle straight. Pin, baste, and tackstitch the pieces in place.

The Holly Leaves, Berries, and Pinecones

1. Position the holly leaves and berries according to the placement guide. Embellish using a stem stitch (page 94) and lazy daisy stitch (page 94).

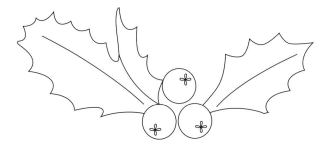

2. Using the placement guide, add the pinecones. Embellish them with a fly stitch (page 94), which will create the textured look of a pinecone.

Embellishment

Add beads to the jacket (see the detail photo under The Beard and Jacket, Step 2, previous page).

tip

Add the beads last because it is easy to catch your thread in them when you are hand sewing.

~ *Hint* ~

When appliquéing these jagged-edged pieces, tackstitch only in between the points. Never try to appliqué a point.

Assemble the Rug

BACK THE RUG

1. Place the rug top on a piece of wool large enough to accommodate the rug base. Baste the 2 pieces securely around the edge, inside the white line.

2. Cut both pieces together just inside the white line so any trace of the line will be removed and your pattern will be accurate.

3. Using a length of white perle cotton #8, stitch the edges of the top and back together with the blanket stitch (page 93).

ATTACH THE PENNIES

1. Carefully place the pennies along the outside edge of the rug and pin them in place.

2. Using basic white sewing thread, baste the pennies in place around the edge of the rug.

3. With white quilting thread, whipstitch the perle cotton threads together, securing the pennies to each other and to the rug base.

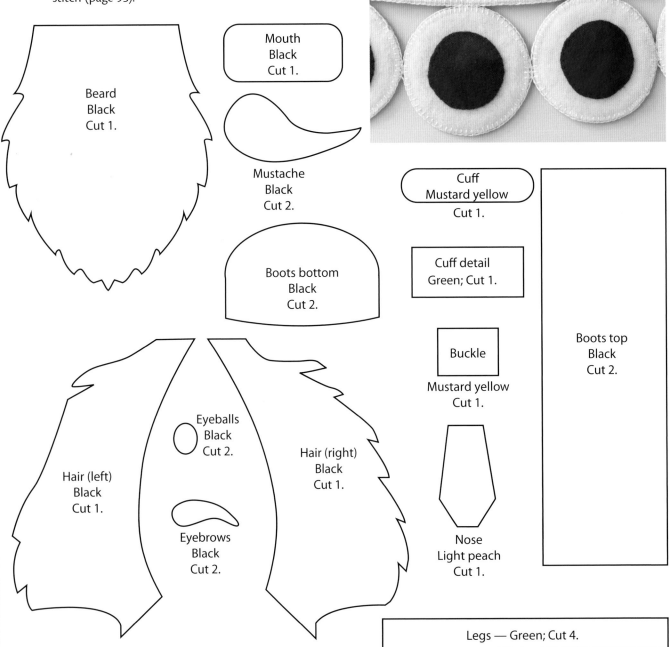

Beard
Black
Cut 1.

Mouth
Black
Cut 1.

Mustache
Black
Cut 2.

Boots bottom
Black
Cut 2.

Cuff
Mustard yellow
Cut 1.

Cuff detail
Green; Cut 1.

Buckle
Mustard yellow
Cut 1.

Boots top
Black
Cut 2.

Hair (left)
Black
Cut 1.

Eyeballs
Black
Cut 2.

Hair (right)
Black
Cut 1.

Eyebrows
Black
Cut 2.

Nose
Light peach
Cut 1.

Legs — Green; Cut 4.

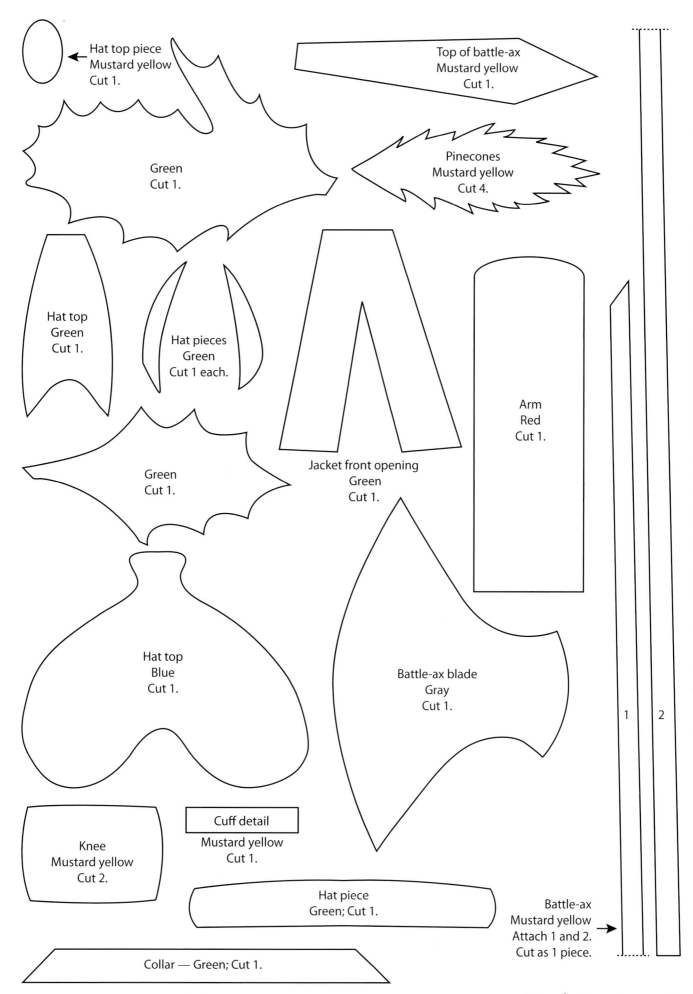

Hat top piece
Mustard yellow
Cut 1.

Top of battle-ax
Mustard yellow
Cut 1.

Green
Cut 1.

Pinecones
Mustard yellow
Cut 4.

Hat top
Green
Cut 1.

Hat pieces
Green
Cut 1 each.

Jacket front opening
Green
Cut 1.

Arm
Red
Cut 1.

Green
Cut 1.

Hat top
Blue
Cut 1.

Battle-ax blade
Gray
Cut 1.

Knee
Mustard yellow
Cut 2.

Cuff detail
Mustard yellow
Cut 1.

Hat piece
Green; Cut 1.

Battle-ax
Mustard yellow
Attach 1 and 2.
Cut as 1 piece.

1   2

Collar — Green; Cut 1.

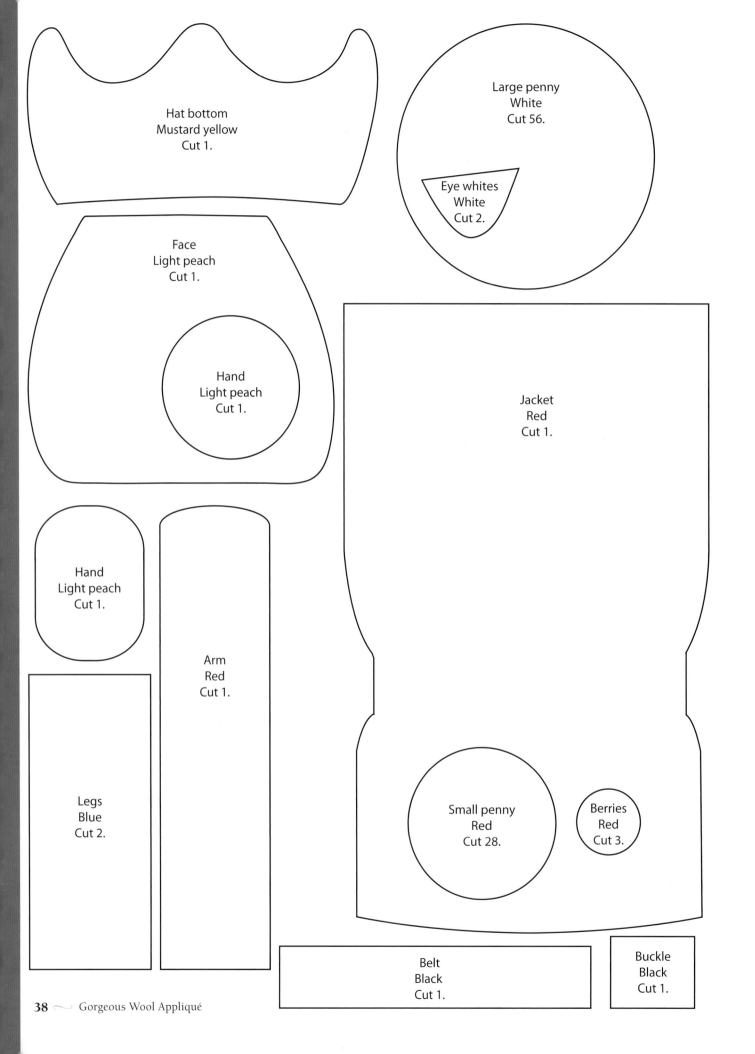

Hat bottom
Mustard yellow
Cut 1.

Large penny
White
Cut 56.

Eye whites
White
Cut 2.

Face
Light peach
Cut 1.

Hand
Light peach
Cut 1.

Jacket
Red
Cut 1.

Hand
Light peach
Cut 1.

Arm
Red
Cut 1.

Legs
Blue
Cut 2.

Small penny
Red
Cut 28.

Berries
Red
Cut 3.

Belt
Black
Cut 1.

Buckle
Black
Cut 1.

Heartsease

Rug

Finished rug:
27″ diameter

Inspiration

This gay wreath of dimensional heartsease (wild pansies) is woven around a circular penny rug surrounded by lamb's ears—a perfect setting for your spring bouquet. The design was inspired by a Polish pottery pitcher that I purchased at a craft fair. The pitcher featured casual brush strokes of vines and pansy blossoms. I have deliberately left the center of the design open for the placement of a vase.

SUPPLIES

- 1 yard black felted wool
- 14″ × 14″ green felted wool
- 10″ × 14″ purple felted wool
- 6″ × 6″ yellow felted wool
- 2 skeins green crewel-weight wool thread
- Yellow and purple wool thread
- Black perle cotton #8
- Template plastic
- Crewel and tapestry needles
- DMC 725 floss (topaz) for flower centers
- DMC 315 floss (black) for pansy embellishment
- Tissue paper
- Clear acetate

Prework

For details on using tissue paper and making guides, see The Basics (page 8).

1. Trace the pattern for the project base onto the flat (not shiny) side of a piece of freezer paper, joining the two halves of the pattern where indicated.

2. Mark the base shape (page 10).

3. Create a placement guide (page 11).

4. Create an embroidery guide (page 12).

Later on, you will create a template for each lamb's ear, as they are all different. Right now, just do the prework for the central design.

Embroider the Vines

1. Using a length of green wool thread, chainstitch the vines over the green stitching guides, making sure your starts and stops will be covered with appliqué shapes.

2. Stem stitch the smaller curls and stems.

Note: Do not embroider the vines that run onto the lamb's ears until the lamb's ears are attached.

tip

Remember to use a length of thread that is only twice the distance from your fingertips to your elbow crease. If you like, thread a few needles so you will be able to develop a rhythm and not have to stop to thread. Wool thread is stressed when it is run through wool fabric, so shorter threads will work better.

MAKE FREEZER-PAPER PATTERNS

1. Trace all the pattern pieces for the petals, leaves, buds, and lamb's ears onto the flat (not shiny) side of the freezer paper.

2. Group the pieces by color so you can iron the shapes of the same color to the selected fabric.

APPLIQUÉ THE BLOSSOMS

1. Find the pieces that make the pansy flower and peel the freezer paper away. Place them according to the placement guide.

2. Pin and baste them in place using white thread that will be easy to see and remove later.

3. Using a length of wool thread that matches the pansy, tackstitch the petals in the order in which they overlap.

4. Repeat Steps 1–3 for each flower.

Embellishment

1. Embellish the flowers with a stem stitch using both black and yellow floss.

2. Complete the flowers by using 2 strands of cotton floss to add 10–15 colonial knots to the center of each.

ADD THE BUDS AND LEAVES

1. Peel and position the buds and leaves according to the placement guide, making sure they overlap the ends of the green chain stitching. Use the placement guide to make sure they are arranged correctly; then use your eye and be sure the placement pleases you.

> ### tip
>
> *For smaller pieces, use a drop of glue to baste and tweezers to position the pieces accurately.*

2. With matching wool thread, tackstitch around the leaves, beginning on the right side of each.

3. When you arrive back at the base, bring the thread up into the stem, slightly below the leaf base, and make an elongated lazy daisy stitch from the stem into the leaf base. This small finishing stitch will make the leaf appear to be naturally growing off the stem.

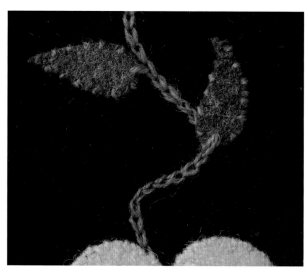

4. Arrange the buds according to the placement guide and tackstitch, making sure the pieces overlap the embroidered stems.

5. Place 3–4 lazy daisy stitches at the base of the bud, carefully fanning them over the base to form a calyx.

6. Complete the appliqué and embroidery for the rug center.

Assemble the Rug

CUT OUT THE TOP AND BASE

1. Position the completed appliquéd rug on top of a square of black felted wool and baste both layers together inside the white line, using white thread, which can be easily seen and removed later. Smooth as you go.

2. Cut the bottom and top pieces out together following the white line.

Note: Cutting both pieces together will be easy. Be sure to cut away the white line and smooth any jagged edges.

You now have the sandwiched rug, and the lamb's ears will slip in between.

ADD THE LAMB'S EARS

Please read all the directions carefully and refer to the illustrations before you begin.

1. Pair the tops and bottoms of all the lamb's ears—the bottoms are the longer pieces, cut using the full pattern outline.

2. For the 10 blank lamb's ears, baste the tops to the bottoms and blanket stitch the edges using black perle cotton #8. Bury your knots between the layers. Set these lamb's ears aside until Step 11 (page 44).

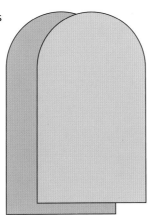

Lamb's ear top and bottom

Note: These are easier to stitch before you attach them to the rug base.

3. Create tissue-paper patterns for each of the 10 lamb's ears with appliqué. Each ear design is slightly different and requires its own pattern and placement guide. Create the tissue patterns for each ear as follows:

    a. Create a master placement tissue pattern of the design like you did with acetate for the center design. Line it up with its corresponding number.

You may need to make little adjustments here to be sure your vines line up.

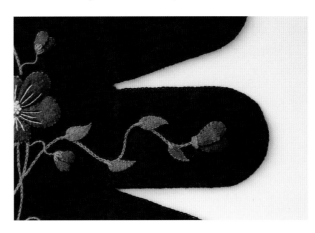

    b. Create a second tissue to use for a stitching guide. Pin this to the lamb's ear top.

4. Using a length of green cotton thread, stitch a running stitch through the tissue, creating a guide for the vine embroidery.

5. Remove the tissue using quick ripping movements toward the line of stitching. (See Creating Embroidery Guides, page 12.)

6. Line up the flat edge of the lamb's ear with the rug base, matching the vine lines. Baste the ear flush to the rug base using white thread. Using a length of black quilting thread, stitch the lamb's ear to the rug base with a herringbone stitch (page 94).

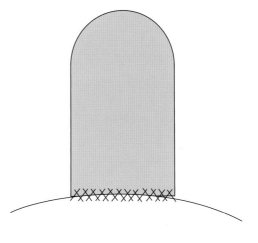

7. Using green wool thread, chainstitch the vines, stitching right over the seam, and appliqué the buds and leaves.

8. Line up the lamb's ear base with the lamb's ear top and slip the base between the rug top and base. Baste these together.

9. Blanket stitch the edges using a length of black perle cotton #8.

10. Repeat Steps 4–9 for each embroidered lamb's ear.

11. Attach the bottom of each of the 20 lamb's ears to the rug base using a herringbone stitch.

Lamb's ear
On black wool, cut 20 using full outline (base)
and 20 using dotted line (top).

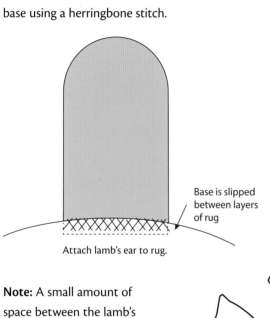

Base is slipped between layers of rug

Attach lamb's ear to rug.

Note: A small amount of space between the lamb's ears is expected and will be inconsequential to the overall design.

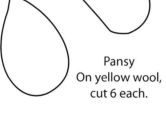

Pansy
On yellow wool,
cut 6 each.

Leaves
On green wool,
cut 10 each.

Pansy
On purple wool, cut 6 each, except 10 each of the A pieces.

THE PILLOWS

Swirling
Tulips Pillow

Finished pillow: 15″ × 15″

Professionally finished by Helene Maszeroski

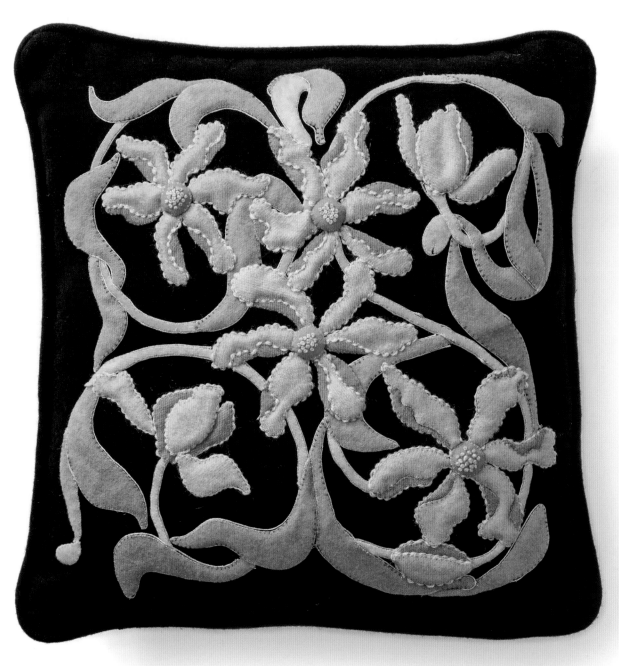

Inspiration

Swirling Tulips is a design inspired by Candice Wheeler (1827–1923), a needle artist, designer, and entrepreneur who contributed greatly to changing the role of women in America. At a time when many women were suffragettes, concerning themselves with the right to vote, Candice was teaching women how to appliqué and create designs that would be commercially viable, offering them an opportunity for economic independence.

I discovered this amazing woman while conducting personal research at the Antonio Ratti Textile Center, the textile lab of the Metropolitan Museum of Art in New York. There I found an appliqué titled *Tulips Panel*, an unfinished work—therefore one never used and well preserved. I had the privilege of studying it closely. As I studied the needlework, even under a magnifying glass, I felt almost as if I knew Candice and her focus on perfection in stitching. And I identified with her. When I discovered that she was an entrepreneur and also founded a school of needlework for women, I was impressed and enamored. I decided to interpret a portion of the design using my own felted wool techniques, and I now share with you this study in creative couching.

SUPPLIES

- Freezer paper for patterns
- Clear acetate for placement guide
- ⅝ yard black felted wool for background, pillow back, and optional piping
- Fat quarter each of Weeks Dye Works felted wool in Meadow, Bubble Gum, Peony, and Lime Green *or* other wool fabric in greens and pinks
- 3″ × 3″ piece of Mustard or other gold felted wool
- Weeks overdyed threads in matching colors
- Krenick braid #002
- Gold thread (Accentuate)
- Paternayan wool yarn to match pink
- Crewel and tapestry needles
- Pink quilting thread
- 16″ zipper
- 15″ × 15″ pillow insert *or* stuffing of your choice

NOTE

Couching is a method of embroidering in which a thread (often heavy), laid upon the surface of the material, is caught down at intervals by stitches taken with another thread through the material.

Prewisork

For details on marking the shapes and making guides, see The Basics (page 8).

1. Prepare the base fabric with the base shape (page 10).

2. Make a placement guide (page 11).

3. Many of the creative couching effects are the result of pulling the needle tight or leaving it loose. Before you begin, study the overlapping objects, and as you stitch, realize that you might have both appliqué and couching happening at once in order to the create the desired look.

⟶ Hint ⟵

Cut the shapes as you progress and key all the pieces to the placement guide in order to stay organized. Have the image and the placement guide readily available for reference as you stitch. At some points you might have unfinished appliqué and couching threads for multiple appliqué pieces.

MAKE FREEZER-PAPER PATTERNS

1. Trace the pieces for the lower left quarter of the design, grouping the pieces of the same color together on a piece of freezer paper. (Refer to Making Freezer-Paper Patterns, page 14.)

Note: This tulip grouping has the least amount of overlapping and will serve as a good starting point to develop confidence. The rest of the design has more overlapping.

2. Press all the patterns onto the appropriate color of felted wool and rough cut the shapes.

Cut and Appliqué

POSITION THE APPLIQUÉ

1. Position the acetate placement guide on the felted wool base, lining up the sides and pinning in place at the top edge. Hinge the placement guide at the top (see Hinging a Guide, page 11).

tip

Don't skip the hinging process. During the project the acetate guide will be removed for stitching and repositioned and pinned to add additional shapes. Using this guide will ensure the accuracy of the design.

2. Cut out the pieces individually and place them aside, ready to position them on the base fabric.

3. Beginning with the lower left quarter of the design, lay and pin the pieces of stems and leaves according to the placement guide.

4. Remove the placement guide, and baste using a milliners needle and white cotton thread in preparation for appliqué.

5. Using the needle-slanting technique (page 16), appliqué these pieces with a tack stitch.

6. Appliqué the main leaf, followed by the underleaf, keeping that piece tight to the main leaf with your thumb as you stitch. Both pieces are appliquéd all the way around.

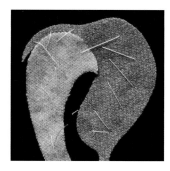

 tip

When the design calls for an underleaf, it will be important to keep that underleaf pushed up tight to the main leaf in order for the leaf to look as if it is merely turning and is all one piece.

ADD THE COUCHED BRAID TO THE LEAF

1. Use a large-eyed crewel needle to begin the braid to be couched. Starting in a nonobvious place, draw up the braid at the beginning of a leaf and secure the cord with a knot. Keep the needle threaded with the cord and rest it out of the way (but ready so you can pull it down at the end of the shape and knot it at the back).

2. Use a straw needle or milliners needle threaded with gold thread to couch the cord—pinned earlier (see Tips, above right, and Note, page 47)—tightly to the shape.

tips

- *To achieve a snug fit, pin the cord tight to the edge and think about trying to use the same hole for both the up and down, securing the stitch close to the edge of the shape.*

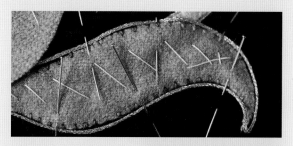

- *To get the leaf tips to curve nicely, use straight pins to position them and then couch closer together.*

ADD THE PETALS

1. Pin the placement guide in place and position the pink petals according to the guide. Pin them in place.

2. Remove the guide and baste the petals in preparation for appliqué.

3. Using the needle-slanting technique (page 16), appliqué these pieces with a tack stitch.

ADD THE COUCHED WOOL THREAD TO THE PETALS

1. Add the couched yarn—2 strands of Paternayan or similar-weight wool thread. Again, use a large-eyed crewel needle to begin the couched threads and secure at the back with a knot.

2. Using pink quilting thread and keeping the couched thread loose, pull the couching thread tight, creating a scalloped look to the edge of the petal. You will see the wool thread puff, creating a sweet scalloped design.

Make the Next Quarters

Repeat all steps of Cut and Appliqué (pages 48 and 49) for each quarter.

As you proceed to appliqué the balance of this design, be careful of the overlapping. On occasion you will see the need to pin back an overlapped piece to complete the couching for another underneath it.

Assemble the Pillow

STUFFED

1. Cut out a square 16″ × 16″ of black felted wool for the back.

2. Line up the pillow top and the pillow back, wrong sides together. Machine sew all the way around, using a ½″ seam allowance and leaving a 4″ opening. Turn the pillow right side out.

3. Stuff with a pillow form or loose poly stuffing or other stuffing of your choice. Sew the opening closed with a whipstitch.

ZIPPERED

1. Cut the black felted wool fabric 16″ × 16″.

2. If you are using piping, prepare it following the instructions in the sidebar. If not, skip to Step 6.

3. Fold 1″ of the loose strip on the piping to the inside and finger-press it. Pin the piping around the outer edge of the front pillow square, right sides together and aligning the raw edges.

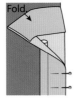

4. Clip into the piping's seam allowance to allow it to curve as you pin the corners.

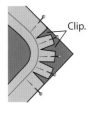

Clip.

5. When you near the starting point, trim the ends of the cord even with each other and close up the piping.

Stop stitching where folded piping starts.

Trim cording where it meets.

6. Pin the closed zipper with the right side facing down onto the right side of the pillow top's bottom edge. The zipper teeth should be even with the cording.

7. Sew the zipper in place using a zipper foot, adjusting the needle position to sew close to the teeth.

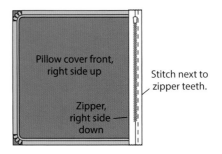

Pillow cover front, right side up

Stitch next to zipper teeth.

Zipper, right side down

8. Fold the zipper tape and seam allowance to the wrong side of the pillow cover.

9. On the pillow back, press under ½″ along an edge. Pin the folded edge of the backing fabric on the zipper next to the teeth and stitch next to the teeth.

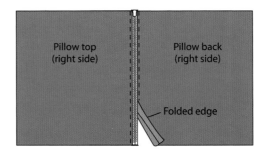

Pillow top (right side)

Pillow back (right side)

Folded edge

10. Unzip the zipper halfway. *Do not* leave it zipped completely—you need to be able to turn the pillow right side out later.

11. Fold the back over the front right sides with the corners and edges lined up. Using a standard sewing foot, start at a corner and sew a ½″ seam around the 3 sides of the pillow that don't have the zipper. Backstitch multiple times over the zipper corners to anchor the zipper.

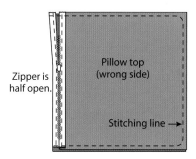

Zipper is half open.

Pillow top (wrong side)

Stitching line →

12. Trim the excess zipper length. Snip the seam allowances of the nonzippered pillow corners at a 45° angle. Turn right side out and press.

tip

An upholstery professional can finish the pillow complete with covered cord and an invisible zipper.

Lime green →

17

18

Green

Piping

Felted wool is stretchy enough that you can make piping with straight strips instead of bias strips.

1. Cut 4 strips of fabric 1½″ × 18″.

2. Sew these strips together end to end, using a ¼″ seam allowance. Press the seams open.

3. Lay the cording in the center of the continuous strip, wrong side up, and fold the fabric over it, keeping the cording in the center and lining up the raw edges of the strip. Pin to hold in place.

4. Leave the first 2″ of the strip unstitched. Using a zipper foot, sew the strip closed so the cording is tightly enclosed. Trim the seam allowance to an even ½″ if necessary.

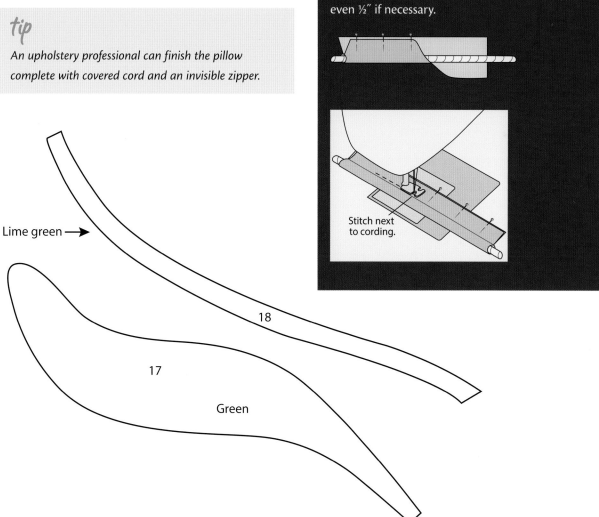

Stitch next to cording.

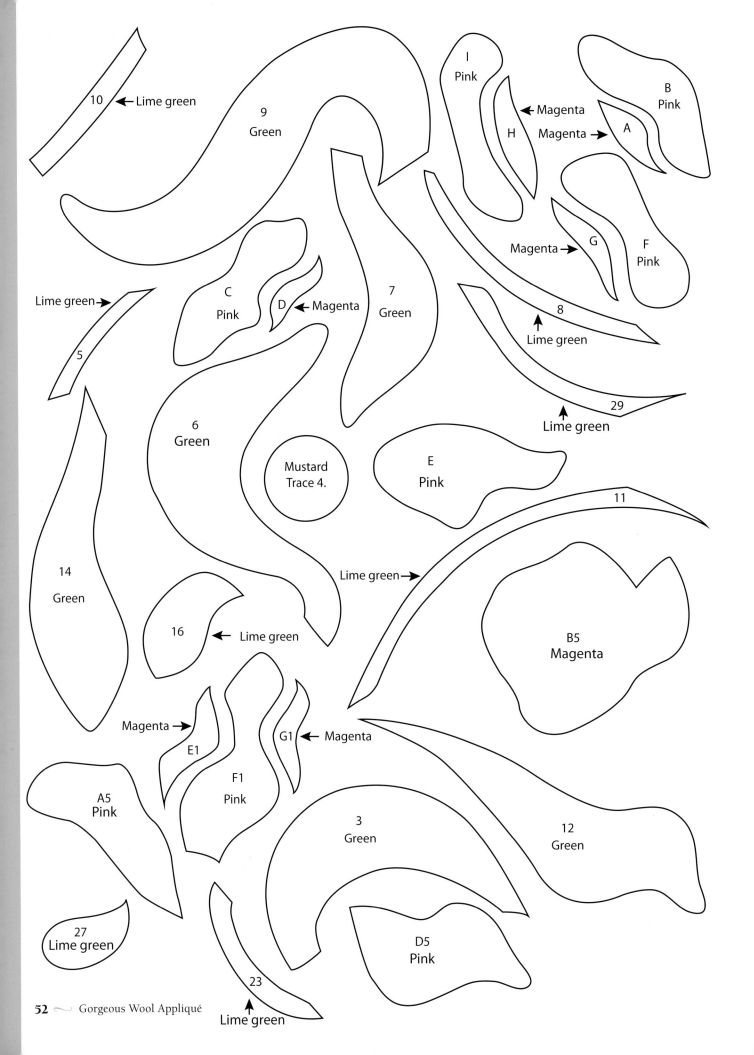

10 ← Lime green

9
Green

I
Pink

← Magenta

H

Magenta → A

B
Pink

Magenta → G

F
Pink

Lime green →

C
Pink

D ← Magenta

7
Green

8

Lime green

5

Lime green

29

6
Green

Mustard
Trace 4.

E
Pink

11

14
Green

16 ← Lime green

B5
Magenta

Magenta →

E1

G1 ← Magenta

F1
Pink

A5
Pink

3
Green

12
Green

27
Lime green

D5
Pink

23

Lime green

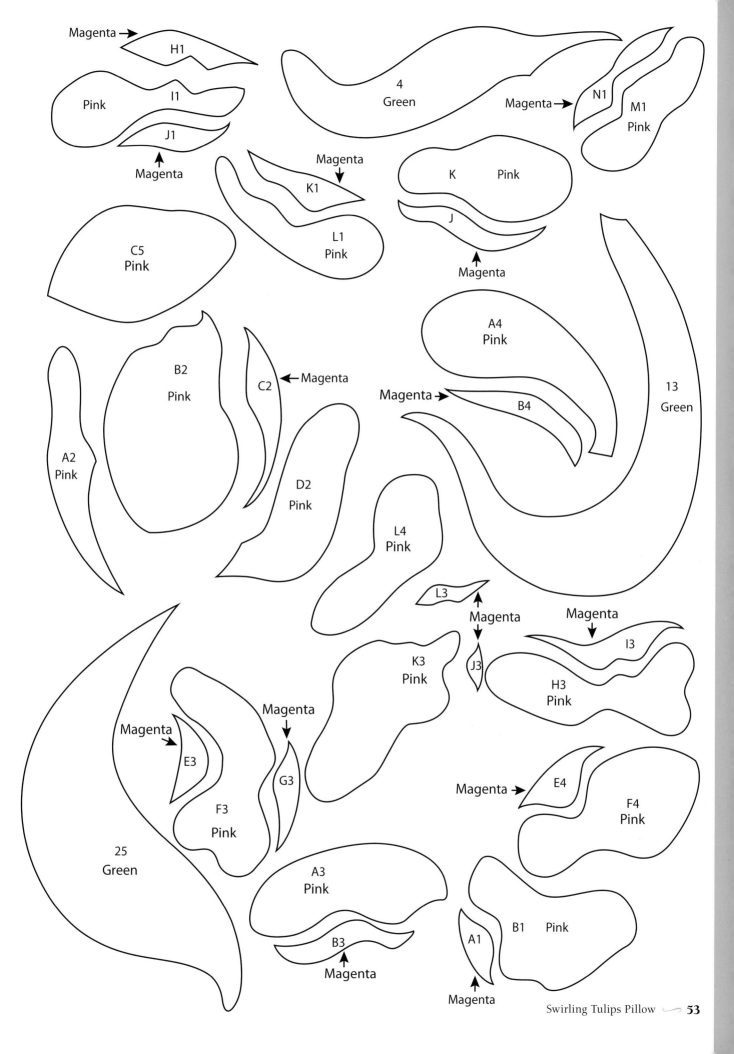

Magenta → H1

Pink I1

J1

Magenta

4
Green

Magenta → N1

M1
Pink

Magenta

K1

Magenta

K Pink

J

L1
Pink

Magenta

C5
Pink

A4
Pink

B2
Pink

C2 ← Magenta

13
Green

Magenta → B4

A2
Pink

D2
Pink

L4
Pink

L3

Magenta

Magenta

I3

Magenta → J3

K3
Pink

H3
Pink

Magenta

Magenta

E3

E4

Magenta → E4

F3
Pink

G3

F4
Pink

25
Green

A3
Pink

B1 Pink

A1

B3

Magenta

Magenta

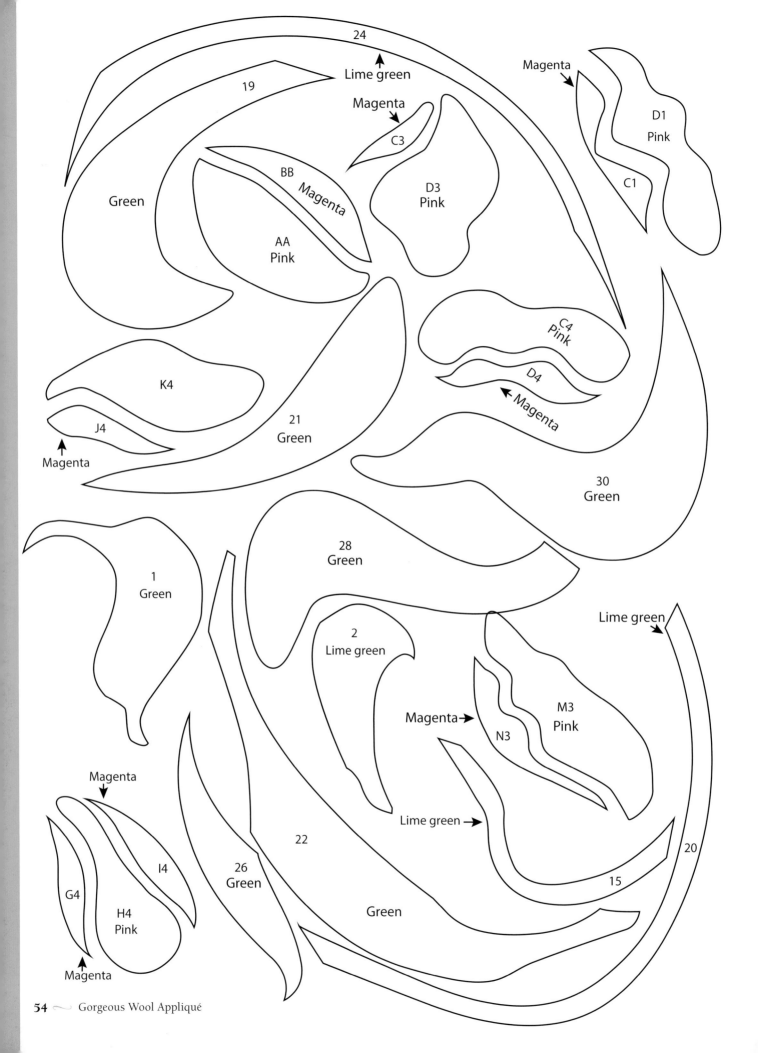

24
Lime green

Magenta

19

Magenta

C3

BB
Magenta

Green

AA
Pink

D3
Pink

D1
Pink

C1

K4

J4

Magenta

21
Green

C4
Pink

D4

Magenta

30
Green

28
Green

1
Green

2
Lime green

Lime green

Magenta →

M3
Pink

N3

Magenta

Lime green →

22

I4

26
Green

G4

H4
Pink

Green

15

20

Magenta

Jacobean
Pillow

Finished pillow: 15″ × 15″

Professionally finished by Helene Maszeroski

Inspiration

Jacobean-era embroidery of the sixteenth century was lyrical and winding in its design and often contained fantasy flowers and fruits. I absolutely love the decorative embroidery of that era, a time when the technology to print fabric was not yet developed, and all the decoration of the royals' and nobles' apparel was done in some form of embroidery. I researched countless fantasy flowers and fruits of the period to create this Jacobean design of my own.

SUPPLIES

- ⅝ yard black felted wool for pillow front, back, and optional piping

- Weeks Dye Works felted wool scraps in the following sizes:

  3½″ × 5″ Electric Blue (light blue)

  4½″ × 4½″ Deep Sea (dark blue)

  9″ × 10″ Collards (dark green)

  3″ × 3½″ Meadow (light green)

  3¾″ × 4¼″ Louisiana Hot Sauce (red)

  3½″ × 4″ Mustard (golden yellow)

  2″ × 3¼″ Lemon Chiffon (pale yellow)

  3¾″ × 3″ Carrot (for carnation—medium orange)

  2 pieces each 3½″ × 4″ Sweet Potato (for carnation—medium-dark orange)

  5″ × 5½″ Citronella (light bronze green)

  4″ × 4″ Merlot (purple)

  2½″ × 4½″ White Maize (medium yellow)

  3½ ″ × 4″ Candy Apple (bright red)

- Gumnut Poppies 679 (olive) silk/wool yarn

- Wool thread such as Tentakulum's Rousseau painter's thread or Kirchner painter's thread in Pomegranate, Aqua, Blue, and Tangerine

- Weeks Dye Works Mermaid perle cotton #5

- Medicis white wool thread or similar

- Light blue cotton thread

- Crewel and tapestry needles

- Tissue paper

- Acetate for placement guide

- 16″ zipper

- 15″ × 15″ pillow insert *or* other stuffing of your choice

- 3 yards ⅜″ cording for piping (*optional*)

Prework

1. Prepare the base fabric (page 10).

2. Make a placement guide (page 11).

3. Make an embroidery guide (page 12).

STITCH A GUIDE FOR THE VINES

1. Using straight pins, line up the tissue-paper pattern to the base wool fabric and pin carefully so as not to rip the tissue.

tip

- *At the beginning and end of each line, use a back-stitch to strengthen the stitches and leave a 1" tail.*

- *Make basting stitches as tiny as possible so you can hide them easily once you begin to stitch over them.*

2. Using a milliners needle and green cotton thread, create a running-stitch guideline through the tissue onto the base wool fabric to mark the position of the main stem.

3. Indicate the other vine lines on the base fabric with small green stitches.

4. Remove the tissue using a quick pulling motion. Rip the tissue toward the stitching line. Use tweezers afterward to remove any pieces of tissue that remain stuck in the stitches.

5. You will embroider or appliqué over the green stitches and hide the guideline stitches completely.

Cut and Appliqué

MAKE FREEZER-PAPER PATTERNS

1. Trace all the pattern pieces for the petals, leaves, fruits, and pennies onto the flat (not shiny) side of the freezer paper. Group the pieces by color so you can iron the shapes of the same color to the selected fabric.

2. Iron the freezer-paper patterns, shiny side down, onto the felted wool.

3. Rough cut the freezer-paper patterns by color, trimming close to, but not on, the cutting line for any piece so you can later trim each piece individually. (This will make cutting more accurate, as you will not have the weight of the fabric yardage pulling.)

4. Use a pair of pinking shears to cut the tops of the carnation petals.

POSITION THE APPLIQUÉ

Position the acetate placement guide on the felted wool base, lining up the sides and pinning in place at the top edge (see Hinging a Guide, page 11).

tip

Don't skip the hinging process. During the project the placement guide will be removed for stitching and repositioned and pinned to add additional shapes. Using this guide will ensure the accuracy of the design.

APPLIQUÉ THE MAIN STEM

1. Find the piece that is the main stem, peel the freezer paper away, and place it along the stitching guide according to the placement and stitching guides.

2. Pin and then baste this main stem in place. This main stem determines the position for the balance of the flowers and fruits in the design, so take time to be accurate.

3. Using a length of wool thread, tackstitch the main stem. It is important to use a light hand, never pulling the work tight, as this piece is slender.

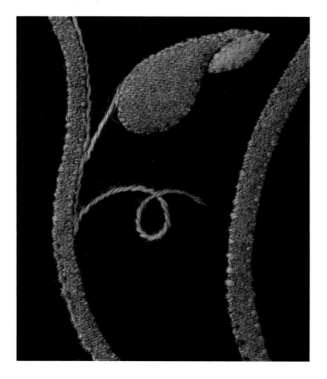

APPLIQUÉ A LEAF

Leaves are constructed using 2 shades of green wool, with the lighter shade indicating the underside of the leaf.

1. Find the 2 pieces that make the leaf that is to the immediate left of the stem base. Peel the freezer paper away and place the pieces according to the placement guide.

2. Pin and baste them in place. Using a length of matching wool thread, tackstitch the dark green leaf first.

3. Place the leaf underside piece snugly against the leaf and tackstitch this piece in place using lighter green thread. Avoid making stitches on the points of any pieces.

4. Embellish. This leaf is embellished using Gumnut 679 yarn along the line between the leaf and the underleaf to smooth the turning transition of the shape.

5. You can choose to appliqué some or all of the remaining leaves now, or wait until the flowers are finished.

APPLIQUÉ THE FANTASY FLOWER

1. Locate the pieces of the fantasy flower. These include mustard, maize, and white for the flower head and green and dark green sepal pieces. Peel the freezer paper away.

2. Layer, pin, and baste according to the placement guide; then stitch.

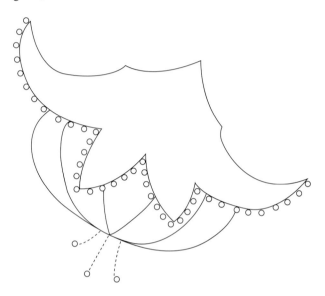

3. Tackstitch the parts of the flower head using matching thread. (I used a variegated one.) Carefully line up the base stem and the flower sepal stem for a smooth transition.

4. Embellish the bronze green sepal closest to the bloom with colonial knots using the Gumnut 679 yarn.

5. Embroider the stamens in white using a stem stitch. Add yellow colonial knots at the ends.

APPLIQUÉ THE BLUE FLOWER

1. Locate the 5 dark blue petals and 5 light blue petal centers and the yellow piece for the flower center. Peel the freezer paper away.

2. Layer the pieces according to the placement guide and baste in place using white thread and a milliners needle. Stitch through all the layers to gain the desired dimensional effect.

3. Tackstitch the outer blue heart-shaped petals first using a matching thread.

4. Tackstitch the top lighter blue petal centers through all the layers.

5. For the flower center, gather the outside edge of the center circle piece using a running stitch and stuff with craft stuffing. Tightly gather the base and tie it off as desired.

6. Add the seed stitches using the Weeks Mermaid perle cotton #5, a variegated thread.

7. Center this piece and slipstitch it to the base using a matching thread (quilting thread is best but any thread will do).

8. Embellish the outside of the flower with elongated lazy daisy stitches in dark blue. Top with colonial knots in yellow.

APPLIQUÉ THE POMEGRANATE

1. Locate the 6 pieces of the pomegranate—the red outside, the red interior, the yellow interior, and the 3 smaller leaves that go at the base. Peel the freezer paper away.

2. Appliqué the red interior piece to the yellow inside piece first, so the yellow piece maintains its round shape.

3. Layer the piece from Step 2 on the red outside piece.

4. Add the 3 leaves at the bottom. Baste and then tackstitch the pomegranate.

5. Embellish it with running stitches to create texture.

EMBROIDER THE STEM TO THE POMEGRANATE

Chainstitch the stem over the guideline from the end of the center stem to the pomegranate. Add a curly vine along the way, using a stem stitch.

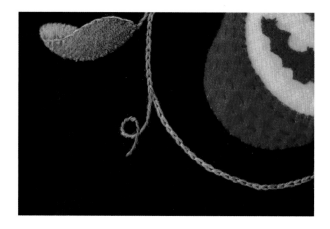

You'll remove any visible guidelines later.

> **NOTE**
> You can chainstitch right next to the guideline, instead of on top of it, and then remove the guideline afterward.

APPLIQUÉ THE CARNATION

1. Locate the pieces of the carnation—3 petals and a sepal. Peel the freezer paper away and assemble the carnation according to the placement guide. Baste.

2. Tackstitch the carnation, making sure to go through all 3 layers on the top petal and leaving the top edge open for added dimension.

3. Tackstitch the sepal using matching thread. Then outline it with the Gumnut 679 yarn along the top edge using a stem stitch.

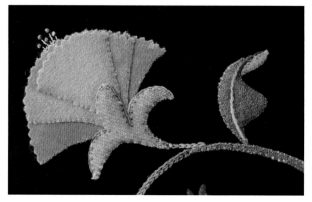

APPLIQUÉ THE GRAPES

1. Locate the leaves and grapes. Peel the freezer paper from the grapes and leaves and position them according to the placement guide. Baste in place. Do not worry about the exact placement of the grapes as long as the grouping pleases you.

2. Tackstitch the grapes and the leaves in place with matching thread.

3. Add clusters of colonial knots on top of some, not all, of the grapes to create dimension.

APPLIQUÉ THE STRAWBERRY

1. Locate the strawberry and leaves, peel the freezer paper away, and baste the pieces in place.

2. Chainstitch the balance of the stems connecting the strawberry and blue flower before tack-stitching the strawberry.

3. Tackstitch the straw-berry and leaves.

4. Embellish the berry with seed stitches using red perle cotton #8.

tip

A chain stitch is used for all the mid-thickness stems. The smaller curling vines are stem stitched to appear thinner.

APPLIQUÉ THE STEMS AND BUDS

Rows of chain stitches gently curve to hold up the budding leaves and flowers.

1. Follow the stitched guidelines.

2. Use a collection of loopy elongated lazy daisy stitches to create a calyx on the blue bud.

APPLIQUÉ THE EDELWEISS

1. Locate the white flowers. Peel the freezer paper away and baste the flowers in place.

2. With matching wool thread, begin at the right side of each petal and tackstitch, finishing off in the center.

3. Add texture with thin "vein" lines of light blue thread on the petals and a yellow colonial knot in the center of each flower.

APPLIQUÉ THE BASE LEAVES

1. Appliqué the remaining base leaves using a tack stitch if you didn't do this at the beginning of the project. Start with the dark green pieces.

2. When adding the second piece, the light-colored piece, press it close to the dark green piece. (See Appliqué a Leaf, page 58.)

3. Repeat Steps 1 and 2 for each leaf.

4. Add a stem stitch to the line between the leaf shapes, using a length of Gumnut 679 yarn, for more clarity. This small finishing stitch will make the leaf appear to naturally turn.

Assemble the Pillow

See Swirling Tulips, Assemble the Pillow (page 50).

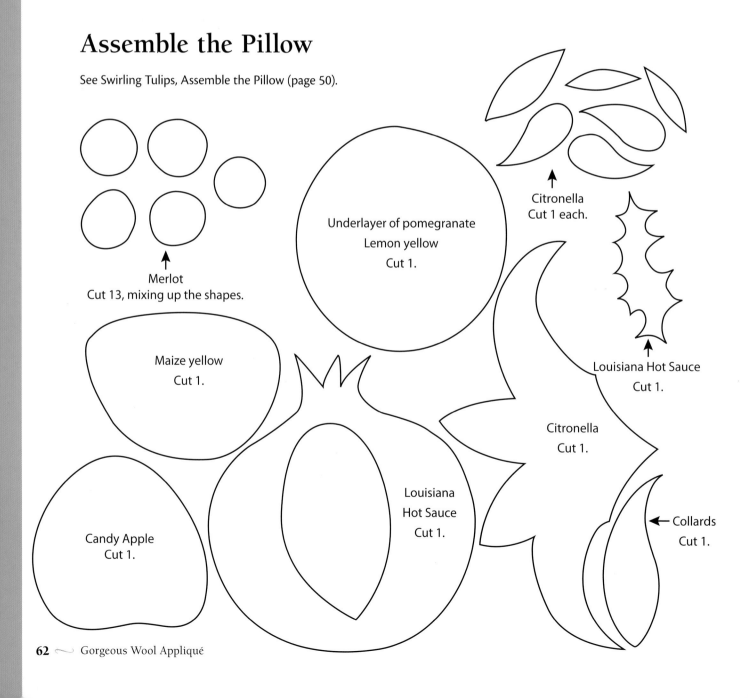

Merlot
Cut 13, mixing up the shapes.

Underlayer of pomegranate
Lemon yellow
Cut 1.

Citronella
Cut 1 each.

Louisiana Hot Sauce
Cut 1.

Maize yellow
Cut 1.

Citronella
Cut 1.

Louisiana
Hot Sauce
Cut 1.

Candy Apple
Cut 1.

Collards
Cut 1.

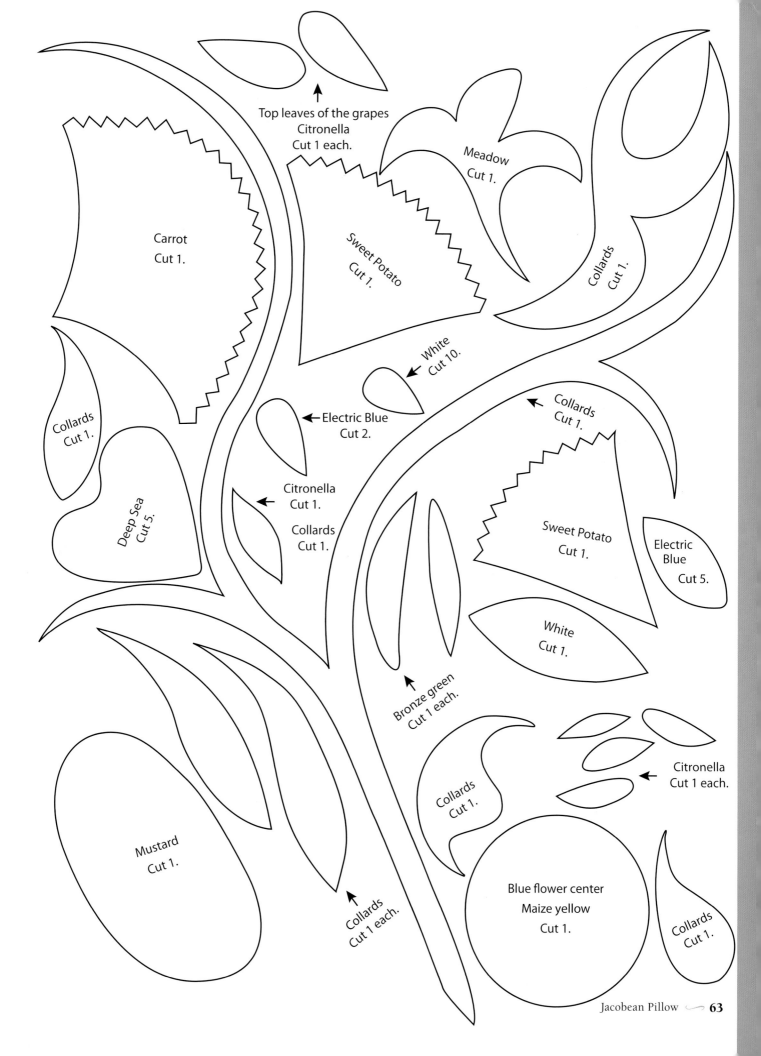

Top leaves of the grapes
Citronella
Cut 1 each.

Meadow
Cut 1.

Carrot
Cut 1.

Sweet Potato
Cut 1.

Collards
Cut 1.

White
Cut 10.

Collards
Cut 1.

Electric Blue
Cut 2.

Collards
Cut 1.

Collards
Cut 1.

Citronella
Cut 1.

Sweet Potato
Cut 1.

Electric
Blue
Cut 5.

Deep Sea
Cut 5.

Collards
Cut 1.

White
Cut 1.

Bronze green
Cut 1 each.

Citronella
Cut 1 each.

Collards
Cut 1.

Mustard
Cut 1.

Blue flower center
Maize yellow
Cut 1.

Collards
Cut 1.

Collards
Cut 1 each.

Celtic
Charm Pillow

Finished pillow: 15″ × 15″

Professionally finished by Helene Maszeroski

Inspiration

This design was taken from the wrought iron hardware design on a great wooden door in the Cloisters, the medieval museum in New York City, which is part of the Metropolitan Museum of Art. I was struck by the bold symmetry and remember sketching the design on a napkin (photos were frowned upon) during my initial visit to the museum. I transferred the design into dimensional felted wool appliqué using the paper-cut method, and then I embellished the appliqué with chain stitching, knots, and needle weaving. I had the piece finished as a throw pillow, and it has become a dramatic focal point in my living room.

SUPPLIES

- ⅝ yard black felted wool for pillow front, back, and optional piping
- Fat quarter of moss green overdyed felted wool
- Overdyed wool thread in moss green
- Overdyed silk thread in yellow green
- Overdyed wool thread in multicolored shades of autumn colors
- Gold perle cotton #8
- Green perle cotton #12

- Crewel needles
- Freezer paper
- Tissue paper
- Basting thread
- Beads
- 16″ zipper
- 15″ × 15″ pillow insert *or* other stuffing of your choice
- 3 yards ⅜″ cording for piping (*optional*)

Prework

For details on marking the base fabric and making guides, see The Basics (page 8).

1. Prepare the base fabric (page 10).

2. Make a placement guide (page 11).

MAKE A PAPERCUT PATTERN

1. Accurately fold a piece of freezer paper (flat side out) into quarters and crease. Then unfold.

2. Within a quarter, line up the pattern (a quarter of the design) with 2 sides of the fold.

3. With a no. 2 pencil, trace the pattern onto the freezer paper.

4. Fold the freezer paper once again in quarters and staple it together securely, making sure to avoid the traced line.

NOTE

This pattern includes *bridges*, which are designed to hold the shape of the appliqué as it is positioned and stitched. Bridges are cut away and removed entirely during the appliqué process.

Bridges

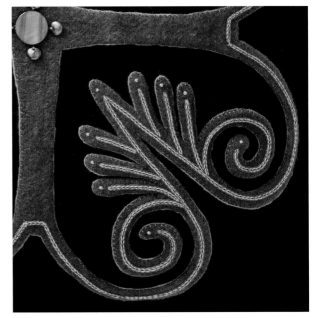

5. Carefully cut out the design and remove the staples. Open the freezer paper flat and you will have completed a 4-corner Celtic design.

6. Position the cutout from Step 5 on the green felted wool, shiny side down, and press with a hot iron.

Cut and Appliqué

1. Using a pair of scissors with a sharp-pointed blade, cut away the appliqué carefully, leaving the bridges in place.

> ## tips
>
> - You might find it easier to snip a cut into the center areas and cut out to the edges, trying to always cut toward a corner.
>
> - Cutting should always leave a smooth line to the design. Don't concern yourself with what you are cutting away or how many pieces or cuts you make. Smooth out any jaggies or inaccuracies once the freezer paper is removed.
>
> - If you accidently cut into a bridge, don't worry; continue cutting but leave the rest of the bridge intact. Take a stitch or two on the miscut area to hold the bridge in place until later.

2. Position the acetate placement guide on the felted wool base and hinge it into place (see Hinging a Guide, page 11).

3. Peel the freezer paper from the green felted wool and position the cutout design in place on the wool base, lining it up with the placement guide. When you are satisfied, pin it securely in place.

4. Using a milliners needle and white basting thread, baste the design to the felted wool base (see Basting Tips, page 18).

5. Using a matching green crewel thread and a crewel needle, appliqué the design using the needle-slanting technique (page 16).

6. As you come to each bridge, cut it away with sharp embroidery scissors and continue to stitch. Keep your pattern handy so you will be able to refer to it to recognize the bridges easily.

EMBELLISH

1. Embellish the entire edge of the design using a stem stitch and an overdyed complementing color of crewel wool thread.

2. Embellish the interior of the design using a chain stitch in gold perle cotton #8.

3. Add the colonial knots at the end of each point.

4. Use green perle cotton #8 to interlace the entire chainstitched design with needle-weaving (page 93).

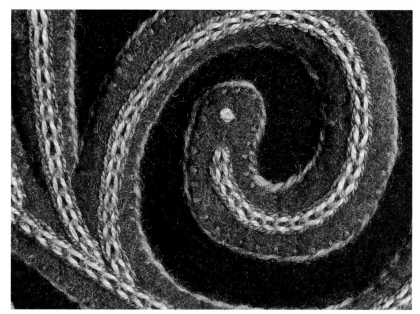

Detail of interlaced chain stitch

5. Add and secure the decorative beads.

Assemble the Pillow

See Swirling Tulips, Assemble the Pillow (page 50).

Do not cut.

Fold line

Bridge ·················

THE SMALLS

Buttercup Pincushion

Finished pincushion: 4″ diameter × 2½″ high

Professionally finished by Kim Hollifield of Round Rock, Texas

As a quilter I use a pincushion a great deal. Once I began to work in felted wool I realized how magnificent it is to needle, and I decided that felted wool would make an excellent pincushion. As for buttercups, I absolutely love them. I have ever since I was a child. I remember holding a blossom under my sister Robin's chin to test the lore—if this causes your skin to light up yellow, then it's empirical proof that you like butter; apparently she loved butter.

SUPPLIES

- 9″ × 14″ black felted wool for background
- 4″ × 6″ yellow felted wool for petals and buds
- 4″ × 6″ green felted wool for leaves
- Black perle cotton #8
- Matching yellow and green wool threads
- Matching yellow and green cotton floss
- Yellow and white perle cotton #8 for flower center embellishment
- Freezer paper for pattern making
- Sewing accessories and crewel and tapestry needles of your choice
- Craft stuffing
- Tissue paper
- White or light-colored gel pen
- Acetate plastic for placement guide
- Template plastic
- BBs or other small weights for added weight

Prework

For details on using tissue paper, marking the base fabric, and making guides, see The Basics (page 8).

1. Prepare the base fabric (page 10).

2. Make a placement guide for the top and side pieces (page 11).

3. Prepare a tissue-paper pattern for the embroidery for the top and sides (page 12).

Make Freezer-Paper Patterns

1. Trace all the pattern pieces for the pincushion—top, bottom, sides, leaves, and petals—onto the flat (not shiny) side of the freezer paper. Group these pieces by color so you will be able to iron the shapes of the same color to the selected fabric. The bottom is cut the same size as the top.

2. Rough cut the freezer-paper patterns by color, trimming close to, but not on, the cutting line for each piece.

3. Cut out the circle for the pincushion top on the cutting line and iron the circle to the black felted wool.

4. Using a white or light-colored gel pen, trace around the freezer-paper circle pattern, giving yourself a clear guide on the base fabric for the top of the pincushion. Iron the freezer-paper patterns, shiny side down, onto the black, yellow, and green felted wool.

5. Cut out all the shapes on the cut lines but do not remove the freezer paper.

Appliqué

1. Remove the freezer paper and baste the shapes for the petals in place on the pincushion top.

2. Use the placement guide to accurately position and pin the pieces. Using white thread and a milliners needle, baste the pieces in place.

3. Using a length of yellow wool thread and the needle-slanting technique (page 16), tackstitch the petals in place.

> **NOTE**
>
> One leaf is actually underneath one of the petals—you can baste it in place before tackstitching the petals.

4. Chainstitch the vines and stems using a length of green wool thread.

5. Using a 12″–18″ length of single-strand yellow embroidery floss, appliqué the buds.

6. Use green wool thread to appliqué the larger leaf.

7. For the 3 smaller leaves, simply use a stem stitch through the center to anchor each. Do not tack the sides.

8. Chainstitch the side vines using a length of green wool thread.

9. Use a 12″–18″ length of single-strand green embroidery floss to appliqué the leaves to the pincushion sides.

Embellish

1. Using a length of gold perle cotton #8, add colonial knots to the flower center. Fill in these gold knots with additional knots in white perle cotton #8.

2. At the center of each petal edge, add a single elongated lazy daisy stitch in gold perle cotton.

3. Using a single length of yellow cotton floss, add lines to the petals to indicate growth.

4. Add stem stitches to the center of each leaf. For help with accuracy, baste a line using green thread and stem stitch over it to be certain the vein lines are placed where you want them.

5. Use a single length of yellow embroidery floss to indicate the petal definition in the buds.

Assemble

With right sides together, fold the side panel in half widthwise and whipstitch it closed, creating a cylinder shape (see Stitch Glossary, page 94). Turn right side out and pin this cylinder to the pincushion bottom. Baste so you can remove the pins. Using a length of black perle cotton #8, buttonhole stitch the closure.

Cut a circular piece of template plastic (slightly smaller than the bottom) and add it to the inside bottom of the pincushion to stabilize it. Then add craft stuffing and some BBs to weight it a bit. Now you can pin and baste the pincushion top and buttonhole stitch the top on.

Sides of pincushion

Cut 4.

Cut 2.

Cut 1.

Cut 2.

B

Top of pincushion

Cut 2.

Cut 2.

Cut 2.

Cut 1.

Cut 1.

Cut 1.

Cut 1.

Cut 1.

A

Attach A and B along the diagonal line and trace the pattern as one piece.

Flowers
from My Beau

Finished sizes:

Pinwheel Pincushion: 3½″ diameter

Tin Box Top: 2½″ × 4″

Scissors Sheath and Fob: 3½″ length

I admit it; I am a hopeless romantic. I love the sweet manners and gifts of the Victorian era and have always been intrigued by the pinwheel pincushions and other vintage sewing accoutrements. I also love Baltimore Album blocks, and I eat a worrisome amount of Altoids mints. These charming little smalls are my answer to making a covered Altoids box, a pinwheel, and a Baltimore Album block, wrapping them in the romance of days gone by.

SUPPLIES

- Freezer paper for pattern making
- Clear acetate for placement guide
- 12″ × 16″ black felted wool total for all items
- 6½″ × 8″ red felted wool
- Miscellaneous scraps of colorful felted wool for flowers and urn
- Red and green wool threads
- Black perle cotton #8
- DMC gold thread

- 10″ length of ⅛″-wide red ribbon for embellishment
- Altoids or similar tin
- Tissue paper
- Crewel, tapestry, straw, and milliners needles
- Glue, such as Roxanne Glue-Baste-It
- 8″ × 8″ scrap of lightweight batting
- 9″ × 12″ sheet of lightweight cardboard

Prework

For details on marking the base fabric and making guides, see The Basics (page 8).

Prepare the base fabric with the base shape for the pinwheel, scissors sheath, and tin top (page 10). Cut the base fabric for the pinwheel about 2″ larger than the pattern all the way around.

MAKE THE PINWHEEL PINCUSHION

Prepare

1. Sew a running-stitch line on the pen line of the base fabric using white thread and a milliners needle. Flip this piece over and use the running-stitch line for your guide.

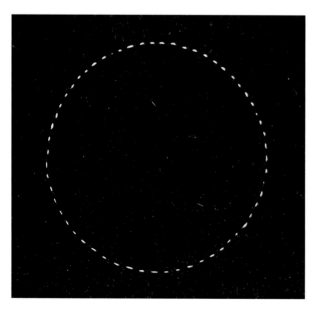

(This will help when assembling the pinwheel because this piece will wrap around the batting and cardboard, and the running-stitch line can easily be removed.)

2. Make a placement guide (page 11).

3. Make an embroidery guide for the flower stems (page 12).

Embroider

Using a single strand of green floss, embroider over the green running-stitch guide using a stem stitch.

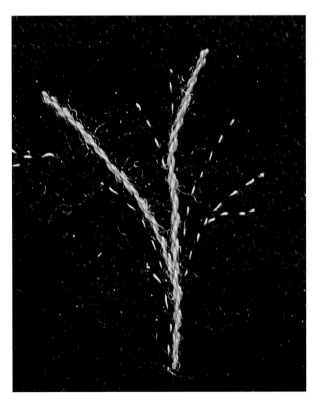

Cutting Techniques

Flower Cutting Technique

Leaf Cutting Technique

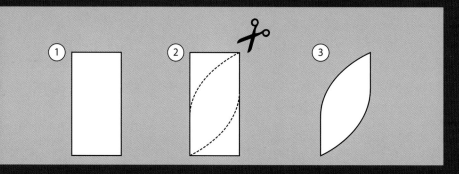

Cut and Appliqué

Refer to Cutting Techniques (on previous page) to see how to cut the small flowers and leaves. The trick here is to cut as indicated and not to attempt to cut as you would normally, around the perimeter of an object.

1. Beginning with the main flowers, cut the leaves and buds. Using tweezers, position them according to the placement guide. Use a tiny dot of glue to hold them in place. Let dry.

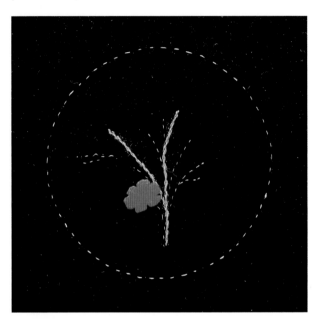

tip

Make sure you wait a sufficient amount of time for the glue to dry before attempting to stitch.

2. Using a length of black quilting thread, sew straight stitches from the flower center toward the outside, indicating the space between the petals and anchoring the flowers.

3. When a single flower is complete, secure the thread using tiny stitches or a knot before moving on to the next flower head.

4. Use the following guides when securing the flowers, leaves, and buds:

- Flowers are embellished with a single colonial knot in the center using a single strand of yellow floss.

- Leaves are appliquéd with a tack stitch using green thread.

- Circular blue flowers are secured with a single colonial knot.

- Triangular flowers are secured with a lazy daisy stitch using green wool thread.

- Orange and blue colonial knots in wool thread create the smallest flower groupings.

- Lazy daisy stitches are used for tiny leaves and sepals.

APPLIQUÉ THE BOW

1. Tie a bow in the red ribbon and adjust it until the loops and tails match the template.

2. Using straight pins, carefully pin the ribbon in place according to the template.

3. Baste the bow in place using white thread and a straw needle.

4. Using red thread and a tack stitch, appliqué the bow in place. Avoid placing stitches on the ends of the ribbon, as this will cause the ribbon to fray.

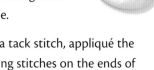

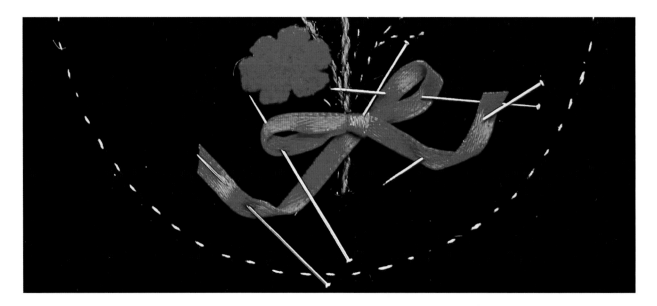

Assemble the Pinwheel

1. From cardboard, cut 2 circles, each 3¼" in diameter.

2. Using a circular cardboard template as a guide, cut 2 circles from the batting. Using a tiny bit of glue, adhere the batting to one side of each cardboard circle.

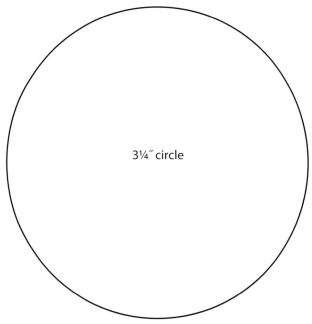

3¼" circle

3. Cut 2 additional circles of batting approximately 1″ larger all the way around.

4. On a fresh piece of cardboard, draw another 3¼″ circle. Draw a line approximately 1″ larger all the way around it. Cut on both of the lines, creating a ring.

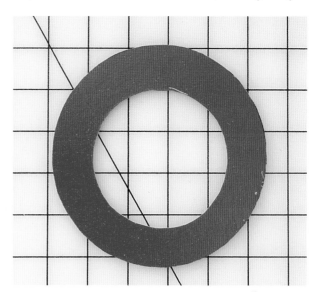

Cardboard/batting assembly (Step 2) and larger batting circle (Step 3)

5. Place the ring on the felted wool appliqué, aligning the white guideline with the center circle. Using a white gel pen, trace around the outside of the ring and cut.

6. Repeat Steps 4 and 5 using a piece of black felted wool for the back.

You should now have 2 batting / cardboard circle assemblies and 2 circles of felted wool to cover them.

NOTE

If you'd like to personalize this project, now is a good time to embroider your name or the recipient's name on the back of the pinwheel.

7. Thread a needle with a double length of black quilting thread. Starting on the right side of the fabric, sew ¼" running stitches about ¼" from the edge of the circle of felted wool with the appliqué. Leave a 3" tail.

8. On the last stitch, bring the needle to the front alongside the first stitch.

9. Turn the fabric circle wrong side up and stack a large-size batting and cardboard / batting assembly on top.

10. Tie an overhand knot and pull the threads to gather the fabric tightly over the cardboard / batting assembly. Tie tightly.

11. Repeat Steps 7–10 for the other circle of wool.

12. Rethread a needle with another double length of thread. Knot the end and secure the end by making a few tiny stitches. Bring the needle up about ⅛" from the edge—this is the "first exit position."

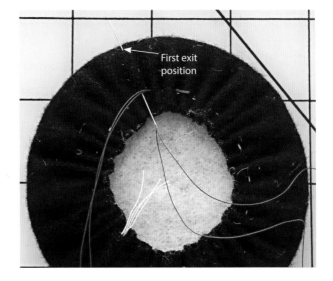

First exit position

13. The 2 sides of the pinwheel are sewn together using a ladder stitch. Hold the pinwheel sides in your left hand with your index finger between them to sew. Stitches should be about ⅛″ from the edge so they will disappear into the felted wool when pulled.

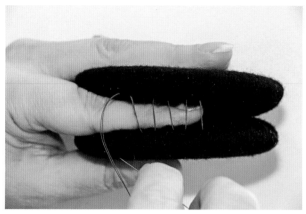

(Reverse this if you are left-handed.)

14. Insert your needle opposite the first exit position and take a ¼″-long stitch. Again, insert the needle opposite the last exit position and take another ¼″ stitch. Aim to create straight thread lines that will line up when linking the 2 sides.

15. About every 6 or 7 stitches, pull the thread tight and the stitches will close up.

16. Sew around the entire perimeter in this manner and then sew a knot to fasten off. Bury the tail and trim the excess thread.

17. Finish by adding red pearlized pins to the edge.

MAKE THE TIN BOX TOP

1. Create a placement guide for the tin top. (See Creating a Placement Guide, page 11.)

2. Create a white running-stitch guide on the black wool for the appliquéd area of the tin top, as marked on the template pattern.

3. Trace the pattern for the urn on the flat (not shiny) side of the freezer paper. Iron it, shiny side down, onto the red felted wool. Carefully cut out the piece. Leave the freezer paper on the wool until you use it.

4. Cut the flowers and leaves. (See Make the Pinwheel Pincushion, Cut and Appliqué, page 81.)

- Leaves and small flowers are appliquéd with a tack stitch using green thread.

- Flower centers, stamens, and snapdragon flowers are created with colonial knots. Use 2 strands for larger knots.

- Sepals are created using lazy daisy stitches in green wool thread.

- Stems are stitched using a stem stitch in green wool thread.

5. Embellish the urn with couching and blanket stitches using a single strand of DMC gold.

6. The urn handles are completed in chain stitch and finished with a colonial knot using red wool thread.

7. Larger flowers are secured using black quilting thread. (See Make the Pinwheel Pincushion, Cut and Appliqué, Steps 2 and 3, page 81.)

Finish the Tin

1. Cut a piece of black wool ¾″ larger than the dimensions of the top of the tin.

2. Paint the outside of the tin lid with glue and smooth the wool onto the top and sides of the lid.

3. Let the glue dry for 24 hours and then carefully trim the excess wool around the bottom of the lid.

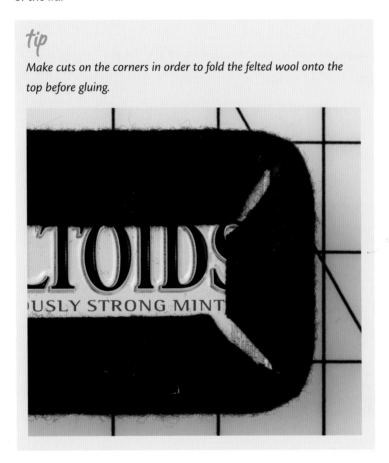

tip

Make cuts on the corners in order to fold the felted wool onto the top before gluing.

4. Cut a strip of black felted wool ½″ wide and long enough to wrap around the side of the tin. Paint the side of the tin with glue and smooth the strip around the tin. Cut the ends flush *after* gluing because the fabric will stretch.

5. Finish the tin top using methods from finishing the pinwheel (see Assemble the Pinwheel, page 82).

- Assemble a piece of batting with 2 pieces of cardboard the size of the tin top.

- Cover that with the appliqué design.

Using a ladder stitch, attach the assembled appliqué / cardboard / batting piece to the wool that you glued to the top of the tin. (See Assemble the Pinwheel, Steps 12–15, pages 84 and 85.)

MAKE THE SCISSORS SHEATH AND FOB

Prepare

1. Create a placement guide for the scissors sheath (see Creating a Placement Guide, page 11). Eyeball the fob; no acetate template is needed.

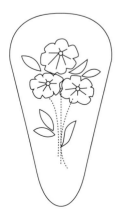 

2. Create a white running-stitch guide on the black felted wool for the appliquéd area of the scissors sheath. These stitches will be removed later.

3. Create a tissue-paper guide for the stems on the scissors sheath (see Creating an Embroidery Guide, page 12).

4. Make twisted cord with 3 strands of black perle cotton #8 to attach the fob to the scissors sheath.

Cut and Appliqué

1. Cut the flowers and leaves. Appliqué. (See Make the Pinwheel Pincusion, Cut and Appliqué, Steps 1–4, page 81.)

> **NOTE**
>
> This is a good project to personalize. Embroider a name or initials on the back of either the sheath or the fob—or both!

2. Baste a piece of red felted wool to one side of each piece of black wool. (Sew the red wool to the back of the appliquéd side.)

3. With red wool sides facing, align the black wool pieces and sew together with black perle cotton #8 using a blanket stitch.

4. For the fob: Sew the red felted wool circle to the back of the fob piece with black perle cotton #8 using a blanket stitch. Tuck the cording between the layers of the fob before the stitching is complete.

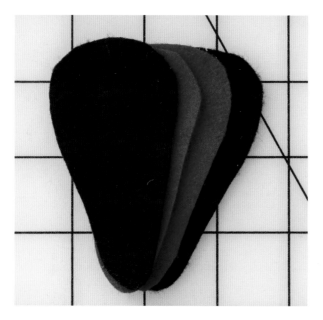

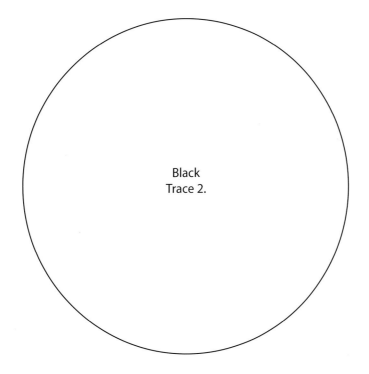

Black
Trace 2.

Black
Trace 2.

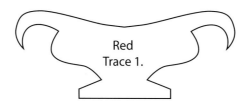

Red
Trace 1.

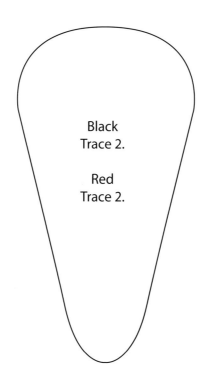

Black
Trace 2.

Red
Trace 2.

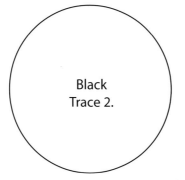

Black
Trace 2.

Stitching Glossary

Basting Stitch

Blanket Stitch

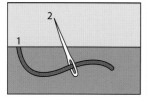 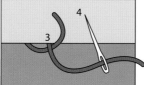

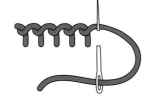

Bullion Stitch

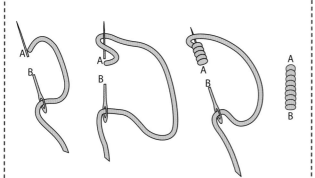

Chain Stitch

Chain Stitch with Needle Weaving

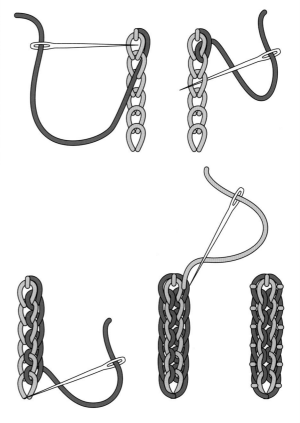

Colonial Knot

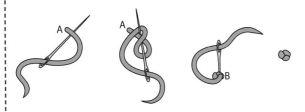

Running Stitch

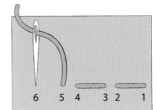

Couching Stitch

Satin Stitch

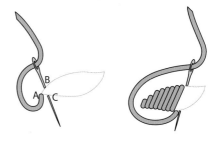

Fly Stitch

Seed Stitch

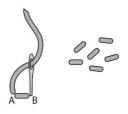

Herringbone Stitch

Stem Stitch

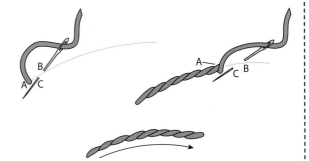

Ladder Stitch

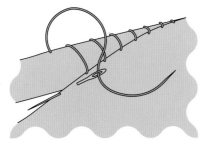

Whipstitch

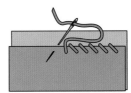

Lazy Daisy Stitch

About the Author

Deborah Gale Tirico is an avid needle artist and trained graphic designer. She has studied appliqué with a variety of prominent teachers and continues to study historical appliqué quilts and coverlets.

Her specialty is the creation of a sculptural look to felted wool appliqué by using needle-slanting techniques and the layering and stuffing of wool pieces. Deborah's designs feature matching and overdyed wool threads and embroidery embellishments, which enhance and define the clarity of her subjects.

Examples of Deborah's work can be found on her website at deborahtirico.com.

RESOURCES

Felted wool	Wool and specialty thread
deborahtirico.com	deborahtirico.com
dorrmillstore.com	kreinik.com
prairiewoolens.com	renaissancedyeing.com
primitivegatherings.us	threadneedlestreet.com
weeksdyeworks.com	threadnuts.com
woolylady.com	tristan.bc.ca
	tristanbrooks.com
	weeksdyeworks.com

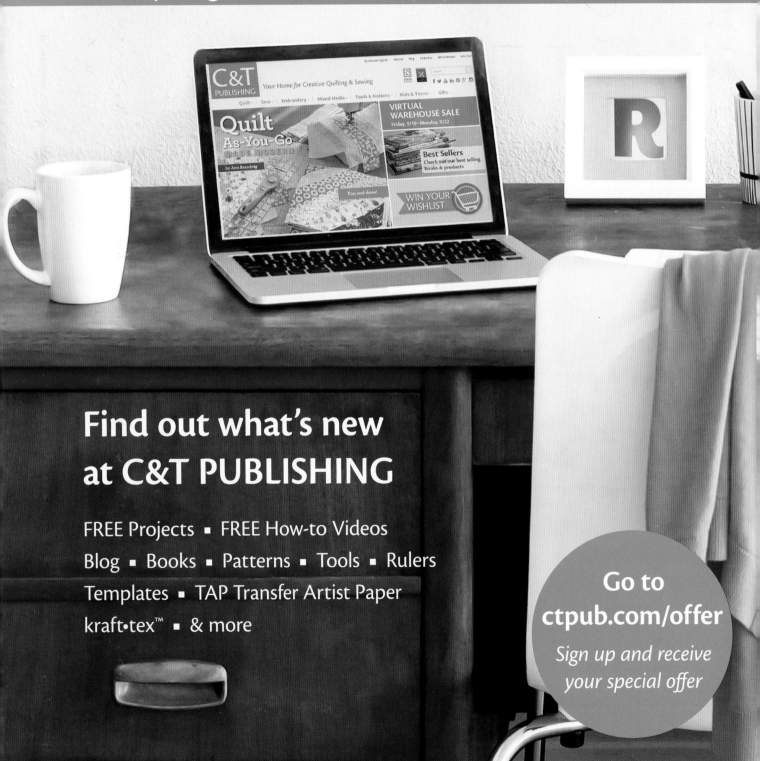